ANIMAL DIVERSITY IN THE FOREST BIOME

ANIMAL DIVERSITY IN THE FOREST BIOME

By

Dr. Amita Sarkar

Deptt. of Zoology
Agra College, Agra
(Uttar Pradesh)
(India)

DISCOVERY PUBLISHING HOUSE PVT. LTD.
NEW DELHI-110 002

Published by:

Tilak Wasan

DISCOVERY PUBLISHING HOUSE PVT. LTD.
4383/4B, Ansari Road, Darya Ganj
New Delhi-110 002 (India)
Phone : +91-11-23279245, 43596064-65
Fax : +91-11-23253475
E-mail : discoverypublishinghouse@gmail.com
sales@discoverypublishinggroup.com
parul.wasan@gmail.com
web : www.discoverypublishinggroup.com

***First Edition:* 2013**

ISBN: 978-93-5056-235-2

Animal Diversity in the Forest Biome

Printed at:
Dynamic Printers
Delhi

Preface

An enormous variety of creatures inhabit the forest. Some are spectacular, others are hidden somewhere beneath the canopy of countless billions of leaves. The web of interactions between individuals and species is intricate and complex; nothing about a forest is simple, and humans are only just beginning to understand any part of these ecosystems.

Forests are some of the most diverse habitats on the planet. Biodiversity is not simply something that's 'nice' to have. All species, including humans, are dependent on all other species for survival. The extinction of even one organism—a monkey, a flowering plant, a water flea—will have unpredictable and often disastrous consequences.

Tropical rainforests are the richest ecosystems in the world. Because of the great diversity of plants and animals, there are actually relatively few individuals of most species. This makes them especially susceptible to habitat loss and other stresses.

While many temperate species have tropical equivalents, there is a greater range of habitats in tropical forests. The warm, moist climate also contributes to the great numbers of species. There are complete groups of tropical rainforest organisms that are absent from areas with cooler climates. One example are the epiphytes — smaller plants that actually grow in the branches of larger trees.

When people think of animals that live in forests, creatures such as bears, eagles, gorillas, tigers are usually what come to mind. Forest plants, other than trees, are often ignored. And many people are unaware of the fact that organisms such as bacteria and fungi are just as important to the forest as the trees themselves.

—Author

Contents

Preface

1. **Introduction** 1
Tropical Rainforest; Defenders at Work; Temperate Deciduous Forest; Temperate Coniferous Forest; Boreal (Taiga) Forest; The Forest Ecosystem

2. **Animals Living in the Subtropical/Tropical Dry Forest Habitat** 9
Carnivores; Even-toed Ungulates; Bats; Dasyuroid Marsupials and Marsupial Carnivores; Flying Lemurs; American Marsupials; Kangaroos, Possums, Wallabies, and Relatives; Hyraxes; Hares, Pikas and Rabbits; Elephant-shrews; Monotremes; Bandicoots and Bilbies; Horses, Rhinoceroses and Tapirs; Primates; Elephants; Rodents; Tree Shrews; Edentates

3. **Species Distribution** 18
Clumped Distribution; Regular or Uniform Distribution; Random Distribution; Species Distribution Model; Abiotic and Biotic Factors; Species Distribution Grids Project; Statistical Determination of Distribution Patterns; Global Warming Effects

4. **Animals in Rainforests Biome** 26
Where are Rainforests?; Strata of the Rainforest; Animals that Live in Rainforests; Tropical Rainforest: Animals; Tropical Rainforest: Animal Adaptations; Leafcutter Ants; Stick Insects; Amazon Rainforest

Animals; Spider Monkey; Golden Lion Tamarin; Sloth; Giant Anteater; Giant River Otter; Capybara; Amazonian Manatee; Toucan; Macaw; Amazon Pink River Dolphin; Electric Eel; Piranha; Black Caiman; Anaconda; Jaguar; Poison Arrow Frog

5. **Animal Life in Boreal Forest [Taiga]** **35**
Climate in the Taiga; Plant Species found in Taiga; Indicator Animal Species; Main Carnivores of the Boreal Forest

6. **Popular Animals that Live in Rainforests** **43**
Insects; Lizards, Reptiles and Amphibians; Birds; Monkeys and Gorillas; Other Creatures; Gorilla (*Gorilla gorilla*) – Central West Africa; Giant Anteater or Antbear – Central and South America; Lesser Malay Chevrotain (*Tragus javanicus*) – S. Asia, Sumatra, Java, Borneo; Siamang Gibbon (*Hylobates syndactylus*) – Malaya and Sumatra; Ocelot (*Felis pardalis*) – Central and South America; Black Tree Kangaroo (*Dendrolagus ursinus*) – New Guinea; Okapi (*Okapia Johnstoni*) – Central Africa; Common Tree-Shrew (*Tupaia glis*) – S. Asia, Sumatra, Java, Borneo; Orang-Utan (*Pongo Pygmaeus*) – Borneo and Sumatra; Malayan Pangolin (*Manis javanica*) – South-east Asia; Javan Rhinoceros (*Rhinoceros sondaicus*) – S. Asia, Sumatra, Java; Slender Loris (*Loris tadirgradus*) – South India and Ceylon; Malayan Tapir (*Tapirus indicus*) – Malaysia; Jaguar (*Panthera onca*) – Central and South America; Snakes; Boas; Pythons; Venomous Species

7. **The Biodiversity of the Rainforests** **54**
The Disappearing Rainforests; The Wealth of the Rainforests; Rainforest Action; The Importance of Rain Forest; The Amazon Rain Forest; The Amazon River; Largest Collection of Plant and Animal Species; Scarring and Loss of Diversity; Driving Forces of Destruction; Logging for Tropical Hardwoods; Fuel Wood and the Paper Industry; The Grazing Land;

Subsistence Farming; Leading the Threat: Governments; Rainforests Pharmacy to the World; Bioprospecting; The Secrets of Rainforests; Indigenous People: A Valuable Resource; But Few Benefits for the Indigenous People

8. **The Importance of Forests** 81
Forest Provides Multiple Benefits; Forests Keep the Environment Pleasant; Conserve Soil; Forests are a Main Source of Oxygen; Forests Influence Local and Global Climate; Forests Supplies Food to Millions of People

9. **The Relationship Between the People and Forests** 86
Forests Occupy Approximately One-third of Earth's Land Area; The Greatest Diversity of Species; Temperate Forest; Forest Biomes Represent the Largest and Most Ecologically Complex Systems

10. **The Wildlife of India** 94
Different Types of Organism; Fauna of India; Recent Extinctions; Fungi of India; Flora of India; Biosphere Reserves

11. **Loss of Forests** 100
Rainforests Cover Two Per cent of the Earth's Surface; Consequences of Deforestation; Causes and Motives for Deforestation; Forests are Destroyed by Inequitable Land Policies; Forests are Cleared for Fuel or Export; Policies Needed to Halt Deforestation; Extinction of Plant and Animal Species; Pollution Leads to a Loss of Species; Illegal Wildlife Trade Causes the Loss of Species

12. **Endangered Animals of the World** 111

Greater Horseshoe Bat – (*Rhinolophus ferrumequinum*); Siberian (Amur) Tiger – (*Panthera tigris* ssp. altaica); Loggerhead Turtle (*Caretta caretta*); Northern Bald Ibis (*Geronticus eremita*); White Tailed Eagle (*Haliaeetus albicilla*); Lion-Tailed Macaque (*Macaca silenus*); Mandarin Duck (*Aix galericulata*); Mountain Gorilla (*Gorilla beringei*); Jackass Penguin (*Spheniscus demersus*); Blue Whale (*Balaenoptera musculus*); Numbat (*Myrmecobius fasciatus*); Komodo Dragon (*Varanus komodoensis*); Golden Lion Tamarin (*Leontopithecus rosalia*); Spectacled Bear (*Tremarctos ornatus*); Californian Condor (*Gymnogyps californianus*); Black-footed Ferret (*Mustela nigripes*); White Rhinoceros; African Wild Asses; Leopards; Gazelles; Giant Pandas; Sumatran Tiger; The Komodo Dragon; Tapirs; The Seladang; The Bird of Paradise; Leatherback Turtles; The Japanese Ibis; Bald Eagle; The California Condor; Polar Bears; Peregrine Falcons; Ibexes; Musk Oxen; Takahe; Koalas; The Scarlet Macaw; The Quetzal; The Vicuna; The Giant Anteater; The Bespectacled Bear; Beginning of Life; Extinction is for ever!; Is it Important to Save Animals From Extinction?; Saving Endangered Animals

13. Wildlife Conservation **140**

Forests Stabilize the Climate; Wildlife Conservation; Major Threats to Wildlife; Hunting and Angling Laws are Created Through the Public Process; Wildlife as an International Resource; Scientific Management of Wildlife

Bibliography **149**

Index **151**

CHAPTER

Introduction

When people think of animals that live in forests, creatures such as bears, eagles, gorillas, tigers are usually what come to mind. Forest plants, other than trees, are often ignored. And many people are unaware of the fact that organisms such as bacteria and fungi are just as important to the forest as the trees themselves.

Inorganic materials are also crucial to the living organisms. Green plants—everything from trees to the most delicate ferns—form the base of all forest ecosystems. These plants require clean air, soil, water, and sun to grow and support the fragile network of life in a forest.

An enormous variety of creatures inhabit the forest. Some are spectacular, others are hidden somewhere beneath the canopy of countless billions of leaves. The web of interactions between individuals and species is intricate and complex; nothing about a forest is simple, and humans are only just beginning to understand any part of these ecosystems.

Forests are some of the most diverse habitats on the planet. Biodiversity is not simply something that's 'nice' to have. All species, including humans, are dependent on all other species for survival. The extinction of even one organism—a monkey, a flowering plant, a water flea—will have unpredictable and often disastrous consequences.

Tropical rainforests are the richest ecosystems in the world. Because of the great diversity of plants and animals, there are actually relatively few individuals of most species. This makes them especially susceptible to habitat loss and other stresses.

While many temperate species have tropical equivalents, there is a greater range of habitats in tropical forests. The warm, moist climate also contributes to the great numbers of species. There are complete groups of tropical rainforest organisms that are absent from areas with cooler climates. One example are the epiphytes — smaller plants that actually grow in the branches of larger trees.

Epiphytes can make up over 50 per cent of the plant species in a tropical rainforest. In the temperate zone, all orchids are found on the ground, while in the tropics there are 20,000 species of epiphytic orchids alone! Epiphytes come in all shapes—hanging, sprawling vines, bushy clumps of water-catching leaves, even cactus-like plants. In some temperate coastal forests, trees are carpeted with layers of epiphytic moss and lichens, but there is nowhere near the variety of plant shapes and sizes as in the tropics.

There is another animal besides humans which can change the forest landscape in powerful and dramatic ways. This animal is a rodent—the. Beavers build dams using trees which they cut down. The dams slow the flow of the streams, creating wetlands and ponds. The wetlands and ponds help prevent flooding and collect rich sediment and organic matter. Beavers favor certain types of trees for their dams, and eventually their less preferred types of trees dominate the forest at the edge ofthe stream

Trees that are dead but still standing are often referred to as 'snags', or, more appropriately, as 'wildlife trees'. These trees are more than a convenient place for woodpeckers to take out their aggressions. When trees die and remain standing, insects such as carpenter ants move in and build nests. Woodpeckers create hollows and cavities in the wood as they search for and eat the insects. These holes are perfect nesting sites for songbirds, which consume pests that are harmful to the forest.

Remove any of these organisms, and the entire ecosystem would collapse. Everything is essential—the snags, the ants, the woodpeckers, the songbirds, even the pests, for without the pests, there would be no snags.

Fruit grows at the ends of branches. The ends of branches are hard to reach, and often too thin to support the weight of an animal such as a monkey. Some animals have come up with a solution: the prehensile tail, which works like an extra arm. Others have taken to gliding through tree tops. These are two adaptations which have evolved in response to the particular characteristics of the animals' forest habitat.

Forests occupy one third of the Earth's land area and are found on all corners of the globe. While there are a few different types of forests, all forests have trees as the dominant plant type.

Forests are divided into three different layers: the forest floor, the understory and the canopy. The forest floor is comprised of soil, dead plants and animals and small plants such as grasses and wildflowers. The understory contains small trees or bushes and is also called the shrub layer. The canopy is made up of the leaves and branches of the trees that dominate the forest.

TYPES OF FORESTS

Tropical Rainforest

Location

The tropical rainforests contain the greatest diversity of species of all biomes on earth. They are found around the equator, between 23.5 degrees N latitude and 23.5 degrees S latitude.

Defenders at Work

Learn more about Defenders of Wildlife's work on National Forests and BLM Lands or on the International Wildlife and Timber Trade.

Climate

Temperatures in tropical rainforests remain between 68 and 77° Fahrenheit all year long. Winter is absent in these forests. Most tropical rainforests receive 100 inches of rain per year.

Soil

Because the temperature is warm and the air moist, decomposition happens at a very fast rate in tropical rainforests. High levels of rainfall often lead to leaching of nutrients from the soil, creating soils that are nutrient poor.

Plants

Trees in the tropical rainforests grow between 82 and 115 feet tall and are typically broad-leafed trees. Other plants include ferns, vines, mosses, palms and orchids.

Animals

Dense growing trees create a thick canopy layer in tropical rainforests that keep the sun from penetrating to the lower layers of the forest. This means that most animals that live here must be adapted to living in the trees. A variety of birds, bats, monkeys, snakes and other animals can be found in tropical rainforests.

Threats

The biggest threat to tropical rainforests is unsustainable forestry practices. Other threats include road construction, clearing land for agriculture and other development activities and climate change.

Temperate Deciduous Forest

Location

Eastern United States and Canada, Western Europe and parts of Russia, China and Japan.

Climate

There are four distinct seasons in temperate deciduous forests and precipitation falls throughout the year, as rain in the spring, summer and fall and snow in the winter. Temperate deciduous forests receive 30-60 inches of rain per year.

Soil

The soil in these forests is very fertile.

Plants

The forest floor in temperate deciduous forests supports mosses, ferns and wildflowers and the understory supports a variety of shrubs and ferns. Maple, oak and birch trees are some examples of the deciduous trees that dominate these forests. There are also small numbers of evergreen trees such as pines and fir.

Animals

Animals living in temperate deciduous forests must be adapted to cold winters. Common species found in temperate deciduous forests include, red fox, hawks, woodpecker and cardinals.

Threats

Acid rain caused by industrial and vehicular emissions poses the biggest threat to temperate deciduous forests. Over time, acid rain damages tree leaves, causes trees to produce fewer and smaller seeds and reduces resistance to disease. Other threats include unsustainable forestry, strip mining and the spread of invasive, non-native species that compete for space and food. Climate change is also a threat.

Temperate Coniferous Forest

Location

Temperate coniferous forests are typically found in coastal areas with mild winters and heavy rainfall or in in-land mountainous areas with mild climates. Examples of where these forests are found are Pacific Northwestern United States and Canada, southwestern South America, Southern Japan, New Zealand and small parts of northwestern Europe (Ireland, Scotland, Iceland and Norway).

Climate

Temperate climate with temperature that fluctuates little throughout the year. High levels of precipitation (50-200 inches per year) cause a moist climate and a long growing season.

Soil

Soils are generally rich with a thick layer of decaying material.

Plants

Evergreen conifers dominate these forests. Due to the high levels of precipitation and moderate temperatures, there is a long growing season, resulting in trees that grow very tall. Dominant tree species found in temperate coniferous forests include cedar, cypress, Douglas fir, pine, spruce and redwood. There are some deciduous trees such as maple, and mosses and ferns are common.

Animals

Examples of animals that live in temperate coniferous forests are, deer, marmot, elk, black bear, salmon, spotted owl, marbled murrelet.

Threats

Unsustainable forestry, road construction and other development related activities are the biggest threat to temperate deciduous forests.

Boreal (Taiga) Forest

Location

This is the northern most forest type and is found between 50 and 60° N latitude. Boreal forests are found in Canada, northern Asia, Siberia and Scandinavia (Denmark, Norway, Sweden, Finland). About two-thirds of the world's boreal forests are found in Scandinavia.

Climate

Boreal forests are characterized by long winters and short summers. Most precipitation is in the form of snow and these forests receive between 15 and 40 inches of precipitation per year.

Soil

Because of cold temperatures, decomposition takes a long time, resulting in thin soil.

Plants

Trees are mostly evergreen and include species such as spruce, fir and pine. The understory is limited because the canopy is so dense.

Animals

Animals found here must be adapted to long, cold winters and usually have thick fur. Deer, moose, elk, caribou, snowshoe hare, wolves, grizzly bears, lynxes and wolverines are some examples.

Threats

Unsustainable forestry, climate change, oil and gas drilling.

Most forests, however different in climate and location, are threatened by unsustainable forestry practices, development and climate change. Because forests cover a vast area of land, cross political boundaries and affect a variety of issues including wildlife, development and water there are a number of laws that impact forests.

The Forest Ecosystem

Forest Ecosystems are responsible for much of our Climate Physiology. The Ecosystem is a core function of a working Forest However, simply planting trees will not create a working Forest Ecosystem. To accomplish that you must have virtually all the plant species that Nature provides from the smallest Flowers through woody shrubs and understory trees. Then you add the Birds, Animals and Insects. Only then will the synergy of these elements begin a working forest ecosystem.

The working Forest Ecosystem is a virtual clean climate machine. It Cleans the air removing particulate matter, it cools the air and adds moisture. The Forests absorb existing air separating the elements freeing and releasing the Oxygen disposing of the minor elements and using the CO_2 for food to grow. Forests release water vapor which rises and forms clouds. The working Forest Ecosystem will correct climate change.

Our Survivor Tree project begins with the endangered species Trees, goes through the entire list of Forest Trees and ends with the collection of Americas Heritage Trees. We locate the specimens, collect the tissue, then produce the seed and forward it to the US Forest Service. They will, choose the species mix and plant the seed. This is our mission.

Our project was conceived to rebuild Americas Forests which it will accomplish, However, you can restore a forest and still not have a working Forest Ecosystem. You can plant the Forest Trees and just wait, say 50 years or so or you can plant (or Seed) all the sub species necessary For a working ecosystem. Therefore we have expanded our mission to include the subspecies in our inventory. Working in our favor is the fact that over 80 per cent of the subspecies can be planted using natural seed which is currently available providing a significant cost savings.

A Forest Ecosystem can be as small as a tiny Forest Pool or as large as the entire Forest A Forest Biome is generally larger like the Desert Biome or the National Forest System Biome A Forest Biome designates the area and generally does not contemplate the workings within which is what halting Climate Change is all about. It is the Trees and the Forest Ecosystem that prduce the Oxygen, Removes the particulate matter, cleans humidifys and cools the Air. The Forest emits Water Vapour which rises and forms the Clouds.

CHAPTER

Animals Living in the Subtropical/Tropical Dry Forest Habitat

Even-toed Ungulates

- Bates' pygmy antelope
- Collared peccary
- Suni
- Elk
- Yellow-backed duiker
- Chinkara
- Banded duiker
- Harvey's duiker
- Blackbuck
- Mountain nyala
- Bongo
- Okapi
- Aders' duiker
- Peter's duiker
- Bay duiker
- Banteng
- Jentink's duiker
- Grey ox
- Sharpe's grysbok
- White-bellied duiker
- Gaur
- Maxwell's duiker
- Nilgai
- Red goral
- Natal duiker
- Chinese goral
- Black duiker
- African buffalo
- Goral
- Black-fronted duiker
- Asian buffalo
- Ogilby's duiker
- Takin

Carnivores

- Margay
- Broad-striped mongoose
- Fossa

- Giant-striped mongoose
- Asiatic wild dog
- Brown-tailed mongoose
- Serval
- Common fox
- Liberian mongoose
- Asiatic jackal
- American jackal
- Arctic wolf
- Side-striped jackal
- Gray fox
- Common otter
- Black-backed jackal
- Asiatic black bear
- Malagasy narrow-striped mongoose
- African wild dog
- Bush dog
- Bay lynx
- Malabar civet
- Owston's banded palm civet
- Geoffroy's cat
- Malayan sun bear
- Asiatic golden cat
- Central american cacomistle
- Malagasy ring-tailed mongoose
- Eyra cat
- Maned wolf
- Cougar
- Brown palm civet
- Hose's palm civet
- Leopard cat
- Aquatic genet
- Rusty-spotted cat
- Guadeloupe raccoon
- African lion
- Nilgiri marten
- African golden cat
- Jaguar
- Falanouc
- Peruvian desert fox
- Leopard
- Jungle cat
- Andean fox
- Spotted hyaena
- Ocelot
- Tiger
- Fanaloka
- Sloth bear
- Brown palm civet

Bats

- Straw-coloured fruit bat
- Madagascan rousette
- Long-tailed fruit bat
- Pel's pouched bat
- Moloney's flat-headed bat
- Azores noctule
- Lesser angolan epauletted fruit bat

- Bate's slit-faced bat
- Sierra leone free-tailed bat
- Gambian epauletted fruit bat
- Medje free-tailed bat
- Ryukyu flying-fox
- Large slit-faced bat
- Wahlberg's epauletted fruit bat
- Desert yellow bat
- Dwarf free-tailed bat
- Banks flying fox
- Southern long-nosed bat
- Hairy slit-faced bat
- Franquet's epauletted fruit bat
- Peterson's free-tailed bat
- Intermediate slit-faced bat
- Spurrell's free-tailed bat
- Duke of abruzzi's free-tailed bat
- Ontong java flying fox
- Mt. gargues pipistrelle
- Javan slit-faced bat
- Railer bat
- Ansorge's free-tailed bat
- Chuuk flying-fox
- Large-eared slit-faced bat
- Trevor's free-tailed bat
- Little free-tailed bat
- White-winged flying fox
- Tiny pipistrelle
- Dwarf slit-faced bat
- Marianas flying fox
- Dar-es-salaam pipistrelle
- Egyptian slit-faced bat
- Trident bat
- Caroline flying fox
- St. aignan's trumpet-eared bat
- Philippine tube-nosed fruit bat
- Heart-nosed bat
- Red fruit bat
- Greater mascarene flying fox
- Copper woolly bat
- Fischer's pygmy fruit bat
- Ornate flying fox
- Fly river trumpet-eared bat
- Little golden-mantled flying fox
- Bismarck's trumpet-eared bat

- Samoa flying-fox
- Spurrell's woolly bat
- Philippine gray flying fox
- Australian false vampire bat
- Sundevall's roundleaf bat
- East african little collared fruit bat
- Percival's trident bat
- Daubenton's free-tailed bat
- Jones's roundleaf bat
- Western naked-backed fruit bat
- Golden-capped fruit bat
- Welwitch's bat
- Indian roundleaf bat
- Aellen's roundleaf bat
- Palawan fruit bat
- Moss-forest blossom bat
- Hog-nosed bat
- Large-eared free-tailed bat
- Luzon fruit bat
- Schneider's leaf-nosed bat
- Hildegarde's tomb bat
- Halcyon horseshoe bat
- Rüppell's horseshoe bat
- Mindanao pygmy fruit bat
- Small-toothed fruit bat
- Guinean horseshoe bat

Dasyuroid Marsupials and Marsupial Carnivores

- Tasmanian tiger
- Atherton antechinus
- Cinnamon antechinus
- Red-tailed phascogale
- Long-nosed antechinus
- Lesser antechinus
- Black-tailed antechinus
- Chuditch
- Red-bellied dasyure
- Northern quoll
- Narrow-striped dasyure
- Eastern quoll
- Spotted-tailed quoll
- Kangaroo island dunnart
- Butler's dunnart
- Chestnut dunnart
- Short-furred dasyure

- Broad-striped dasyure
- Three-striped dasyure
- Banded anteater
- Speckled dasyure

Flying Lemurs

- Flying lemur

American Marsupials

- Western woolly opossum
- Bare-tailed woolly opossum
- Central american woolly opossum
- Water opossum
- Pale-bellied woolly mouse opossum

Kangaroos, Possums, Wallabies, and Relatives

- Green ringtail possum
- D'albertis ringtail possum
- Dusky pademelon
- Goldon ringtail possum
- Prosperine rock wallaby
- Great-tailed triok
- Fergusson island striped possum
- Koala
- Leadbeater's possum
- Doria's tree kangaroo
- Black-spotted cuscus
- Long-footed potoroo
- Goodfellow's tree kangaroo
- Huon tree kangaroo
- Scott's tree-kangaroo
- Lemuroid ringtail possum
- Bernard's wallaroo
- Parma wallaby
- Black dorcopsis wallaby
- Macleay's dorcopsis
- Northern hairy-nosed wombat
- Lesser forest wallaby
- Bear cuscus

Hyraxes

- Eastern tree dassie

Hares, Pikas and Rabbits

- Sumatran rabbit
- Tres marias cottontail
- Mexican cottontail

Elephant-shrews

- Golden-rumped elephant shrew
- Black and rufous elephant shrew
- Checkered elephant shrew
- Four-toed elephant shrew

Monotremes

- Long-beaked echidna

Bandicoots and Bilbies

- Long-nosed echymipera
- Eastern barred bandicoot
- Striped bandicoot
- Mouse bandicoot
- Giant bandicoot
- Ceram bandicoot
- Papuan bandicoot
- Raffray's bandicoot
- Golden bandicoot
- Bilby
- Clara bandicoot
- Common echymipera

Horses, Rhinoceroses and Tapirs

- Sumatran rhinoceros
- Javan rhinoceros

Primates

- Javan gibbon
- Allen's bushbaby
- Allen's swamp monkey
- Bornean gibbon
- Hairy-eared dwarf lemur
- Milne-edwards's sportive lemur
- Capped gibbon
- Light-necked sportive lemur
- Greater sportive lemur
- Lesser weasel lemur
- Fork-marked dwarf lemur
- Goeldi's marmoset
- François's langur
- Gee's golden langur
- Crested mangabey
- Bonneted langur
- Collared mangabey
- L'hoest's guenon
- Common langur
- Colombian night monkey
- Indri
- Aye-aye
- Golden bamboo lemur

- Golden angwantibo
- Broad-nosed gentle lemur
- Angwantibo
- Ruffed lemur
- Lesser slow loris
- Bear macaque
- Avahi
- Assam macaque
- White-faced langur
- Crab-eating macaque
- Gray leaf monkey
- Rhesus macaque
- Mitred leaf monkey
- Pig-tailed macaque
- Long-tailed langur
- North sumatran leaf monkey
- Douc langur
- Crowned lemur
- King colobus
- Garnett's greater galago
- Red-bellied lemur
- Olive colobus
- Elegant galago
- Northern needle-clawed bushbaby
- Eastern red colobus
- Diademed sifaka
- Agile gibbon
- Long-nosed monkey
- Verreaux's sifaka
- Ring-tailed lemur
- Dwarf gibbon
- Common gibbon

Elephants

- African elephant

Rodents

- Red bush squirrel
- Fraternal hill rat
- Bocage's mole rat
- Mentawai long-tailed giant rat
- Heinrich's hill rat
- Loring's rat
- Damara mole rat
- Long-headed hill rat
- Major's tufted-tailed rat
- Lord derby's flying squirrel
- Allen's hylomyscus
- White-tipped tufted-tailed rat
- Pel's flying squirrel
- Kondana soft-furred rat
- Siberut flying squirrel
- Angolan hylomyscus
- Webb's tufted-tailed rat

- Mindoro climbing rat
- Particoloured flying squirrel
- Mozambique thicket rat
- Bartel's flying squirrel
- Woodland thicket rat
- Richmond's squirrel
- Smoky flying squirrel
- Long-footed water rat
- Palawan flying squirrel
- Kellen's dormouse
- Sanborn's squirrel
- Fly river water rat
- Sipora flying squirrel
- Savanna dormouse
- Sumatran flying squirrel
- Malagasy giant rat
- Voalavoanala
- Sulawesi soft-furred rat
- Long-eared flying squirrel
- Ranee mouse
- Long-nosed luzon forest mouse
- Lesser ranee mouse
- Mt isarog shrew-mouse
- Mentawi flying squirrel
- Sody's tree rat
- Delacour's marmoset rat
- Koopman's pencil-tailed tree mouse
- Marmoset rat
- Striped ground squirrel
- Servant mouse
- Gray-bellied pencil-tailed tree mouse
- White-bellied luzon tree rat
- Brooke's squirrel
- Pygmy mouse
- Jentink's squirrel
- Phillips's mouse
- Isarog striped shrew-rat
- Alfaro's rice rat
- Blazed luzon shrew rat
- Large-toothed hairy-tailed rat
- Northern palawan tree squirrel
- Peter's mouse
- Luzon striped rat
- Bolivar rice rat
- Culion tree squirrel
- Elegant rice rat
- Namdapha flying squirrel
- Crump's mouse
- Palawan montane squirrel
- Komodo rat
- Yungas rice rat

- Samar squirrel
- White-toothed brush mouse
- Four-striped ground squirrel
- Southern palawan tree squirrel
- Niobe ground squirrel
- Palm rat
- Greater big-footed mouse
- Mentawai three-striped squirrel
- Selinda veld rat
- Dinagat bushy-tailed cloud rat
- Indian giant squirrel
- Liberian forest hybomys
- Betsileo short-tailed rat
- Bocage's rock rat
- Giant bushy-tailed cloud rat
- Grizzled giant squirrel
- Rosevear's lemniscomys
- Peters' hybomys
- Gregarious short-tailed rat
- Red rock rat
- Ilin bushy-tailed cloud rat
- Guinea multimammate mouse
- Typical lemniscomys
- Kaiser's rock rat
- Natal multimammate mouse
- Secretive dwarf squirrel
- Nyika rock rat
- Guinea gerbil
- Celebes shrew rat
- Weber's dwarf squirrel
- Jungle palm squirrel
- Heavenly hill rat
- Kemp's gerbil
- Northern luzon shrew rat

Tree Shrews

- Nicobar tree shrew
- Bornean smooth-tailed tree shrew
- Madras tree shrew

Edentates

- Northern naked-tailed armadillo
- Chacoan naked-tailed armadillo
- Greater naked-tailed armadillo
- Southern long-nosed armadillo
- Common long-nosed armadillo
- Screaming hairy armadillo

CHAPTER

3

Species Distribution

Species distribution is the manner in which a biological taxon is spatially arranged. Species distribution is not to be confused with dispersal, which is the movement of individuals away from their area of origin or from centers of high population density. A similar concept is the species range. A species range is often represented with a species range map. Biogeographers try to understand the factors determining a species' distribution. The pattern of distribution is not permanent for each species. Distribution patterns can change seasonally, in response to the availability of resources, and also depending on the scale at which they are viewed. Dispersion usually takes place at the time of reproduction. Populations within a species are translocated through many methods, including dispersal by people, wind, water and animals. People are one of the largest distributors due to the current trends in globalization and the expanse of the transportation industry. For example, large tankers often fill their ballasts with water at one port and empty them in another, causing a wider distribution of aquatic species.

Clumped Distribution

Clumped distribution is the most common type of dispersion found in nature. In clumped distribution, the distance between neighboring individuals is minimized. This type of distribution is found in environments that are characterized by patchy resources. Clumped distribution is the most common type of dispersion found in nature because animals need certain resources to survive, and when these resources become rare during certain parts of the year animals tend to 'clump' together around these crucial resources. Individuals might be clustered together in an area due to social factors such as selfish herds and family groups. Organisms that usually serve as prey form clumped distributions in areas where they can hide and detect predators easily.

Other causes of clumped distributions are the inability of offspring to independently move from their habitat. This is seen in juvenile animals that are immobile and strongly dependent upon parental care. For example, the bald eagle's nest of eaglets exhibits a clumped species distribution because all the offspring are in a small subset of a survey area before they learn to fly. Clumped distribution can be beneficial to the individuals in that group. However, in some herbivore cases, such as cows and wildebeests, the vegetation around them can suffer, especially if animals target one plane in particular.

Clumped distribution in species acts as a mechanism against predation as well as an efficient mechanism to trap or corner prey. African wild dogs, *Lycaon pictus*, use the technique of communal hunting to increase their success rate at catching prey. It has been shown that larger packs of African wild dogs tend to have a greater number of successful kills. A prime example of clumped distribution due to patchy resources is the wildlife in Africa during the dry season; lions, hyenas, giraffes, elephants, gazelles, and many more animals are clumped by small water sources that are present in the severe dry season. It has also been observed that extinct and threatened species are more likely to be clumped in their distribution on a phylogeny. The reasoning behind this is that they share traits that increase vulnerability to extinction because related taxa are often located within the same broad geographical or habitat types where human-induced threats are concentrated. Using recently developed complete phylogenies for mammalian carnivores and primates it has been shown that the majority of instances threatened species are far from randomly distributed among taxa and phylogenetic clades and display clumped distribution.

Regular or Uniform Distribution

Less common than clumped distribution, uniform distribution, also known as even distribution, is evenly spaced. Uniform distributions are found in populations in which the distance between neighboring individuals is maximized. The need to maximize the space between individuals generally arises from competition for a resource such as moisture or nutrients, or as a result of direct social interactions between individuals within the population, such as territoriality. For example, penguins often exhibit uniform spacing by aggressively defending their territory among their neighbors. Plants also exhibit uniform distributions, like the creosote bushes in the southwestern region of the United States. *Salvia leucophylla* is a species in California that naturally grows in uniform spacing. This flower releases chemicals called terpenes which inhibit the growth of other plants around it and results in uniform distribution. This is an example of allelopathy, which is the release of chemicals from plant parts by leaching, root exudation, volatilization, residue decomposition and other processes. Allelopathy can have beneficial, harmful, or neutral effects on surrounding organisms. Some allelochemicals even have selective affects on surrounding organisms; for example, the tree species *Leucaena leucocephala* exudes a chemical that inhibits the growth of other plants but not those of its own species, and thus can affect the distribution of specific rival species. Allelopathy usually results in uniform distributions, and its potential to suppress weeds is being researched. Farming and agricultural practices often create uniform distribution in areas where it would not previously exist, for example, orange trees growing in rows on a plantation.

Random Distribution

Random distribution, also known as unpredictable spacing, is the least common form of distribution in nature and occurs when the members of a given species are found in homogeneous environments in which the position of each individual is independent of the other individuals: they neither attract nor repel one another. Random distribution is rare in nature as biotic factors, such as the interactions with neighboring individuals, and abiotic factors, such as climate or soil conditions, generally cause organisms to be either clustered or spread apart. Random distribution usually occurs in habitats where environmental conditions and resources are consistent. This pattern of dispersion is characterized by the lack of any strong social interactions between species. For example; When dandelion seeds are dispersed by wind, random distribution will often occur as the seedlings land in random places determined by uncontrollable factors. Tropical fig trees exhibit random distribution as well because of wind pollination. In addition to tropical fig trees and dandelion seeds, oyster larvae can travel hundreds of kilometres powered by sea currents, which causes random distribution when the larvae land in random places. Although random is thought to be unpredictable, it is the only dispersion that has a mathematical equation to represent it. This is due to the individualistic characteristics of random dispersion based on the idea that every species has equal opportunity and access to resources.

Species Distribution Model

Species distribution can now be potentially predicted based on pattern of biodiversity at spatial scales. A general hierarchical model can integrate disturbance, dispersal and population dynamics. Based on factors of dispersal, disturbance, resources limiting climate, and other species distribution, predictions of species distribution can create a bioclimate range, or bioclimate envelope. The envelope can range from a local to a global scale or a density independence to density dependence. The hierarchical model takes into consideration of requirements and impacts or resources as well as local extinctions in disturbance factors. Models can integrate the dispersal/migration model, the disturbance model, and abundance model. SDM's can be used to assess climate change impacts and conservation management issues. Species distribution models include, presence/absence models, the dispersal/migration models, disturbance models, and abundance models. A prevalent way of creating predicted distribution maps for different species is to reclassify a land cover layer depending on whether or not the species in question would be predicted to habit each cover type. This simple SDM is often modified through the use of range data or ancillary information- such as elevation or water distance.

Recent studies have indicated that the grid size used can have an effect on the output of these species distribution models. The standard 50 × 50 km grid size can select up to 2.89 times more area than when modeled with a 1 × 1 km grid for the same specie. This has several effects on the species conservation planning under climate change predictions (global climate models- which are frequently used in the creation of species distribution models- usually consists of 50-100 km size grids) which could lead to over-prediction of future ranges in species distribution modeling. This can result in the misidentification of protected areas intended for a specie's future habitat.

Abiotic and Biotic Factors

The distribution of species into clumped, uniform, or random depends on different abiotic and biotic factors. Any non-living chemical or physical factor in the environment is considered an abiotic factor. There are three main types of abiotic factors: climatic factors consist of sunlight, atmosphere, humidity, temperature, and salinity; edaphic factors are abiotic factors regarding soil, such as the coarseness of soil, local geology, soil pH, and aeration; and social factors include land use and water availability. An example of the effects of abiotic factors on species distribution can be seen in drier areas, where most individuals of a species will gather around water sources, forming a clumped distribution.

Biotic factors, such as predation, disease, and competition for resources such as food, water, and mates, can also affect how a species is distributed. A biotic factor is any behaviour of an organism that affects another organism, such as a predator consuming its prey. For example, biotic factors in a quail's environment would include their prey (insects and seeds), competition from other quail, and their predators, such as the coyote. An advantage of a herd, community, or other clumped distribution allows a population to detect predators earlier, at a greater distance, and potentially mount an effective defense. Due to limited resources, populations may be evenly distributed to minimize competition, as is found in forests, where competition for sunlight produces an even distribution of trees.

There are three basic types of population distribution within an area. From top to bottom:

1. uniform;
2. random; and
3. clumped.

Biogeography is the study of the distribution of biodiversity over space and time. It is very useful in understanding species distribution through factors such as speciation, extinction, continental drift, glaciation, variation of sea levels, river capture and available resources. This branch of study not only gives a description of the species distribution, but also a geographical explanation for the distribution of particular species. The traditional biogeographic regions were first modeled by researchers *'The Geographical Distribution of Animals'*. These were based on the work of Sclater's terrestrial biogeographic regions. Wallace's system was based on both birds and vertebrates, including non-flying mammals, which better reflect the natural divisions of the Earth due to their limited dispersal abilities.

Species Distribution Grids Project

The Species Distribution Grids Project is an effort led out of the University of Columbia to create maps and databases of the whereabouts of various animal species. This work is centered on preventing deforestation and prioritizing areas based on species richness. As of April 2009, data are available for global amphibian distributions, as well as birds and mammals in the Americas. The map gallery contains sample maps for the Species Grids data set.

Statistical Determination of Distribution Patterns

There are various ways to determine the distribution pattern of species. The Clark-Evans nearest neighbor method can be used to determine if a distribution is clumped, uniform or random. To utilize the Clark-Evans nearest neighbor method, researchers examine a population of a single species. The distance of an individual to its nearest neighbor is recorded for each individual in the sample. For two individual that are each other's nearest neighbor, the distance is recorded twice, once for each individual. To receive accurate results, it is suggested that the number of distance measurements is at least fifty.

However, many researchers believe that species distribution models based on statistical analysis, without including ecological models and theories, are too incomplete for prediction. Instead of conclusions based on presence-absence data, probabilities that convey the likelihood a species will occupy a given area are more preferred because these models include an estimate of confidence in the likelihood of the species being present/absent. Additionally, they are also more valuable than data collected based on simple presence or absence because models based on probability allow the formation of spatial maps that indicates how likely a species is to be found in a particular area. Similar areas can then be compared to see how likely it is that a species will occur there also; this leads to a relationship between habitat suitability and species occurrence.

Global Warming Effects

Researchers from the Arctic Ocean Diversity (Arcod) project have documented rising numbers of warm-water crustaceans in the seas around Norway's Svalbard Islands. Arcod is part of the Census of Marine Life, a huge 10-year project involving researchers in more than 80 nations that aims to chart the diversity, distribution and abundance of life in the oceans. Marine Life has become largely affected by increasing effects of global warming. This study shows that as the ocean temperatures rise species are beginning to travel into the cold and harsh Arctic waters. Even the Snow Crab has extended its range 500 km north.

CHAPTER 4

Animals in Rainforests Biome

Rainforests are very dense, warm, wet forests. They are havens for millions of plants and animals. Rainforests are extremely important in the ecology of the Earth. The plants of the rainforest generate much of the Earth's oxygen. These plants are also very important to people in other ways; many are used in new drugs that fight disease and illness.

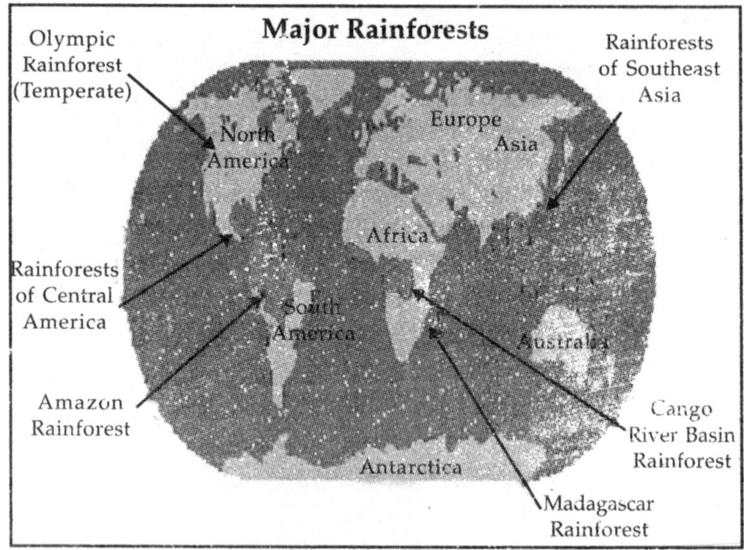

Fig. 4.1: Major Rain Forests

Where are Rainforests?

Tropical rainforests are located in a band around the equator, mostly in the area between the Tropic of Cancer (23.5° N latitude) and the Tropic of Capricorn (23.5° S latitude). This 3000 mile (4800 km) wide band is called the 'tropics'. Tropical rainforests are found in South America, West Africa, Australia, southern India, and Southeast Asia.

Strata of the Rainforest

Different animals and plants live in different parts of the rainforest. Scientists divide the rainforest into strata (zones) based on the living environment.

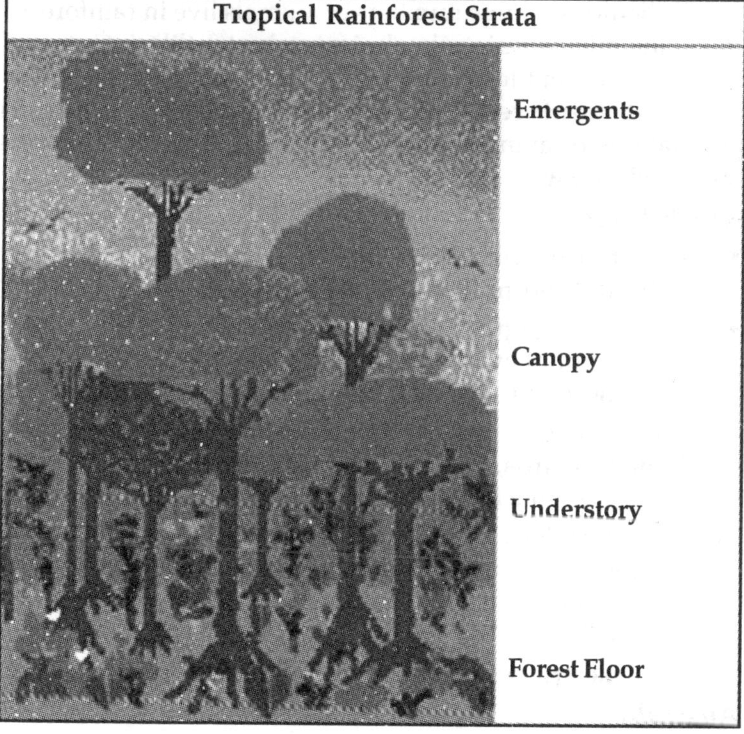

Fig. 4.2: Strata of the Rainforest

Starting at the top, the strata are:

- **Emergents:** Giant trees that are much higher than the average canopy height. It houses many birds and insects.
- **Canopy:** The upper parts of the trees. This leafy environment is full of life in a tropical rainforest and includes: insects, birds, reptiles, mammals, and more.
- **Understory:** A dark, cool environment under the leaves but over the ground.
- **Forest floor:** Teeming with animal life, especially insects. The largest animals in the rainforest generally live here.

Animals that Live in Rainforests

Ridiculously huge numbers of animals live in rainforests, including microscopic animals, invertebrates (like insects and worms), fish, reptiles, amphibians, birds, and mammals. The different rainforests of the world support different populations of animals. A few animals from each rainforest are listed below:

South America

- Insects (morpho butterfly, Julia butterfly, Monarch butterfly, and millions of other insects).
- Mammals (jaguar, ocelot, didelphid opossums, sloth, howler monkey, spider monkey, capybara, many bats, marmosets, procyonids, peccaries).
- Birds (quetzal, macaw, tinamous, curassows, hoatzins, hummingbirds, eagles, ovenbirds, antbirds, flycatchers, puffbirds, toucans, jacamars, tanagers, tapirs, troupials, honeycreepers, cardinal grosbeaks, xenops).
- Reptiles (anaconda, caiman, iguanas, lizards, microteiid lizards, boas, and coral snakes), amphibians (poison arrow frog, etc.).
- Fish (electric eel, piranha), and millions of other animals.

Australia

- Mammals (tree kangaroo, rat kangaroo, yellow-footed Antechinus, Giant White-tailed Uromys, opossums, bandicoot, echidna, duck-billed platypus, sugar glider, red legged pademelon).

- Birds (cassowary, brolga, emerald dove, orange-footed scrubfowl, Australian brush-turkey, sarus crane, gray goshawk, wompoo fruit dove, topknot pigeon, Australian king parrot, laughing kookaburra, lesser sooty owl, fernwren, barred cuckoo-shrike, golden whistler, etc.)
- Reptiles (frilled lizard, carpet python, Green Tree Snake, Spotted Tree Monitor, Eastern Water Dragon, Boyd's Forest Dragon, Northern Leaf Tailed Gecko).
- Insects (Ulysses butterfly, Zodiac Moth, Union Jack butterfly, Regent skipper, Birdwing Butterfly).
- Amphibians (Giant Tree frog, Striped marsh frog, Northern Barred frog, Dainty Green Tree frog), and millions of other animals.

Southeast Asia

- Mammals (tarsiers, orangutans, Siamangs, gibbons, colobine monkeys, tigers, tree shrews, binturong, moonrats, most flying foxes, colugos, bamboo rats, Oriental dormice).
- Birds (tree swifts, leafbirds, fairy bluebirds, fantails, whistlers, flowerpeckers, wood swallows).
- Insects (Queen Alexandra's Birdwing butterfly, Goliath Birdwing butterfly, Saturn Butterfly), and millions of other animals.

West Africa

- Mammals (antelopes, bonobo, chimpanzee, gorilla, Mandrill, scaly-tailed squirrels, otter shrews, duikers, okapi, hippopotamus, Cercopithecus monkeys, bushbabies, pygmy hippo, duiker).
- Birds (Congo peafowl, African Gray Parrot) and millions of other animals.

Tropical Rainforest: Animals

There are billions of species (kinds) of mammals, insects, birds and reptiles found in tropical rainforests. There are so many that there are many that have not been named or even identified yet.

About half of all the world's animal species live in tropical rainforests, in all the layers of the forest. Different animals are found in different countries.

It is estimated that there are more than 50 million different kinds of insects alone in tropical rainforests. Almost 50 different species of ant were found on *one* tree in Peru.

Tropical rainforests are almost perfect for animal survival. It is always warm, and there are no season changes bringing times when there is little food. There is shade from the heat and shelter from the rain. There is no shortage of water.

Tropical Rainforest: Animal Adaptations

Because there are so many creatures living in the rainforest, there is a great deal of competition for food, sunlight and space. Animals have developed special features in order to survive. This is called adaptation.

Some animals became very specialised. This means that they adapted to eating a specific plant or animal that few others eat. For example, parrots and toucans eat nuts, and developed big strong beaks to crack open the tough shells of Brazil nuts.

Leafcutter Ants

Leafcutter ants climb tall trees and cut small pieces of leaves which they carry back to their nest.The leaf pieces they carry are about 50 times their weight.The ants bury the leaf pieces, and the combination of the leaves and the ants' saliva encourages the growth of a fungus, which is the only food these ants eat.

Sometimes there are relationships between animals and plants that benefit both. Some trees depend on animals to spread the seeds of their fruit to distant parts of the forest. Birds and mammals eat the fruits, and travel some distance before the seeds pass through their digestive systems in another part of the forest.

One problem with specialisation is that if one species becomes extinct, the other is in danger too unless it can adapt in time. One example is that of the dodo and the calvaria tree. The dodo, a flightless bird of Mauritius, became extinct in 1681. Today there are just 13 *calvaria* trees left on the island, each over 300 years old, and nearly at the end of their life. Scientists realised that the seeds had to pass through a dodo's digestive system before they could germinate (begin to grow). It seemed that the tree species would also become extinct, but scientists tried domestic turkeys and have successfully managed to germinate some seeds. Many rainforest animals use camouflage to 'disappear' in the rainforest.

Stick Insects

Stick insects are perfect examples of this. There are some butterflies whose wings look like leaves. Camouflage is of course useful for predators too, so that they can catch prey that hasn't seen them. The Boa Constrictor is an example of a camouflaged predator.

The South American three-toed sloth uses camouflage and amazing slowness to escape predators. Green algae grows in the sloth's fur, which helps camouflage it in the forest canopy. Sloths are among the slowest moving animals of all (inside too, as it takes about a month to digest food). They hang from branches in the canopy, and are so still that predators such as jaguars don't see them.

Some animals are poisonous, and use bright colours to warn predators to leave them alone. There are several species of brightly coloured poison arrow frogs. Native Central and South American tribes used to wipe the ends of their arrows onto the frog's skin to make their arrows deadly poisonous.

Amazon rainforest is home to many strangest looking, largest and smallest, loudest and quietest, more dangerous and least frightening animals on Earth.

In fact, both the Andes mountain range and the Amazon rainforest are home to more than half of the world's species of flora and fauna.

The following list of Amazon rainforest animals:

- in no particular order;
- is an introduction to some of the most beautiful;

- most dangerous in some cases; and
- criatures of the jungle.

Your next adventure travel to South America or jungle trekking experience will be better prepared and more enjoyable overall by getting acquainted with them.

Amazon Rainforest Animals

Tremendously reach in animal life, the jungle is populated by insects, arachnids, reptiles, amphibians, birds and mammals. Here are some of them.

Spider Monkey

Inhabits the canopy of the rainforest eating fruits, seeds and leaves. It can grow up to two feet tall, excluding the tail. The spider monkey likes to hang upside down using only its powerful tail to hold on to branches. Other species include: squirrel monkey, capuchin monkey, woolly monkey, red hawler monkey and pigmy marmoset.

Golden Lion Tamarin

A type of monkey of the omnivore typle, the golden lion tamarin eats fruits, insects, spiders, lizards, etc. It can reach up to 12 inches long (with a 12 inches tail) and a weight of about 2 pounds.

Sloth

Lives in the Amazon rainforest canopy, rarely climbing down from the trees. Have huge, hooked claws and long arms. The sloth eats mainly fruits, leaves and bugs, spending most of the time hunging upside down.

Giant Anteater

Armed with a two foot long tongue, the anteater can swallow ants and termites very fast. An adult can reach up to 8 feet long and a weight up to 140 pounds.

Giant River Otter

A highly endangered specie of the Amazon river, it can grow up to 6 feet long and a weight of around 70 pounds. Biggest of its kind in the world, the giant river otter eats mostly fish, small reptiles and birds.

Capybara

Biggest rodent on Earth, the capybara it's about two feet tall and a weight of around 100 pounds. An excelent swimmer, even under water, lives and sleeps in the water, showing only its nostrils above water level. Another endangered specie in the Amazon river. Its diet consist mainly of grass, aquatic vegetation, melons and squashes.

Amazonian Manatee

The largest of all marine mammals found in the Amazon river and its tributaries. An adult manatee can reach up to three metres long and 450 kg in weight.

Toucan

Inhabits the canopy of the Amazon rainforest. With short, thick neck, the toucan is distinguished by its large and colourful beak (black, blue, red, white or combinations). It can grow from about seven inches to over two feet.

Macaw

Largest of the parrot family, the macaw has a sharp, hooked bill ideal for eating nuts, fruits and seeds. It can reach from 1 foot to 3 feet in size, like the Hyacinth macaw. The scarlet macaw - like most of tropical rainforest macaws - is endangered due to poaching, hunting and destruction of habitat through deforestation. Its lifespan is about 75 years in captivity.

Amazon Pink River Dolphin

One of the most beautlfl creatures of the Amazon river, surrounded by all kinds of myths and legends in the jungle.

Electric Eel

A type of fish - not eel at all - that can grow to about 8 feet long and weight of up to 60 punds. Visit Amazon River Fish for more on the electric eel.

Piranha

Perhaps the most feared criature in the Amazon river. It has a powerful jaw and razor-like triangular teeth that can shred flesh from bone in a matter of seconds.

Black Caiman

The largest predator in the Amazon river. It has no enemies other than man and can eat from piranha, capybara and giant river otters to humans. The black caiman can grow to 20 feet long and reach up to 3,000 pounds in weight.

Anaconda

Snake of the boa constrictor type, the anaconda continue to grow throughout its entire life, reaching up to 21 feet long and an astonishing 40 stone of mass. It will squeeze its pray until it cannot breathe, then swallow it, not chewing at all. From capybara to humans, the anaconda doesn't eat often, as it will take more than a week to digest, according to the size of the prey.

Jaguar

One of the most dangerous animals in the Amazon rainforest. An excelent hunter able to swim after pirarucu or turtles climb trees or run after its prey. The jaguar is about 6 feet long and can reach up to 250 pounds in weight.

Poison Arrow Frog

Very small in size, but poisonous enough as to kill up to 100 people It has the most powerful poison known by man, but harmless if left alone. Amazon indians hunt using its poison in the tip of their arrows.

CHAPTER

Animal Life in Boreal Forest [Taiga]

Climate in the Taiga

Climate in the taiga is cold, with average annual temperatures from about +5° to –5° C. It is always find it interesting to note that one location with a coniferous forest, Yellowstone National Park in Wyoming, has an average annual temperature of only 1° C Precipitation varies, from about 20 cm of precipitation per year to over 200 cm. Much of the precipitation, of course, is in the form of snow. The winters are cold and long; summers are relatively short and cool. With snowmelt and low temperatures, there is little evaporation in the summer, so the ground is usually very moist during the growing season. Add to the availability of water the fact that the short summer has extremely long day length at the northerly latitudes and you have a situation for explosive plant growth in the summer. Still the growing season is short, usually less than three months.

The boreal forest, also known as Taiga, a Russian word that recognizes the swampy nature of much of this forest in the summer, lies to the south of the tundra and to the north of deciduous forests and grasslands. There is no comparable zone in the southern hemisphere, probably because there is little land area there with the proper climate (cold temperatures in the southern hemisphere being moderated

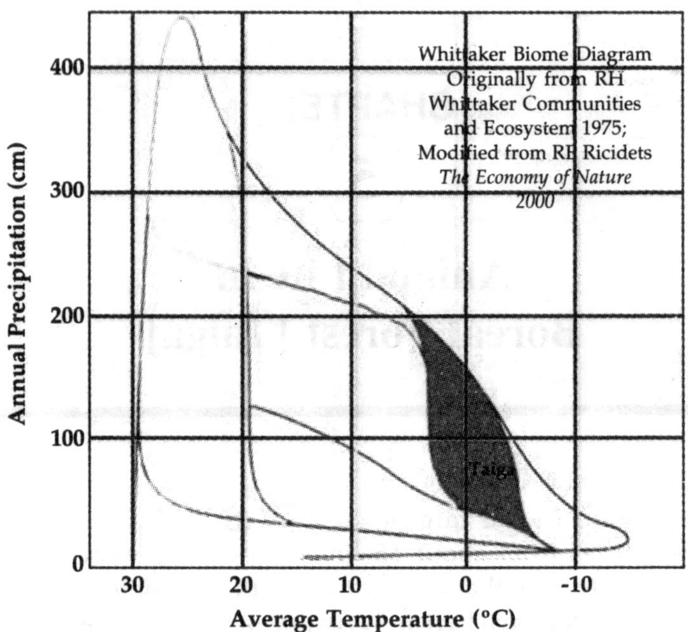

Fig. 5.1: Climate Change in Boreal Forest

by close proximity to the sea; at high latitudes in the southern hemisphere most land is relatively close to the ocean, unlike the northern hemisphere. Also, circulation of the oceans in the southern hemisphere is not blocked by the continental land masses to the same extent as it is in the north. It should be noted that a similar coniferous forests exist on some mountains of the alpine biome; on this map the southern extension of the boreal forests into eastern North America along the Appalachian Mountains is shown, while the coniferous forests of the western North American mountains is not.

Plant Species found in Taiga

Many plant species are found in Taiga, but coniferous trees are obviously the dominant plant form. These trees shed snow easily, and they retain their needles through the winter. The needles themselves are well-adapted, with thick waxy coatings and small surface area, to resist cold conditions and minimize water loss, an important consideration even in the swampy taiga where water may be frozen much of the year. Together, these adaptations mean that even in cool conditions, if the temperature rises above freezing during the day photosynthesis can proceed. Broadleaf plants usually lose their leaves at the onset of freezing conditions in the fall and will not regrow them until most of the danger of frost has passed. This means that the growing season of broad-leafed trees is much shorter than it is for coniferous trees, and the advantage the coniferous trees gain allows them to dominate in the cold taiga climate (note that broad leaves are much more efficient, so if conditions are favorable (warm and moist) they are the preferred leaf type).

Important conifer types include firs and pines (right, with the fir on the left of the image and the pine on the right), spruces, hemlocks, and larches. All of these tree types bear cones of one sort or another. The seeds are retained in these structures until they open and cast the seeds out, often from a considerable height. Some species of birds and mammals may also open the cones foraging for the seeds. With two seeds per scale, it is likely that as the animal breaks one seed loose the other will fall free to the forest floor. Some cones do not open until there has been a fire, but since fire is not an important aspect of the taiga that is probably not the case for most taiga conifers.

Giant Sequoia (*Sequoiadendron giganteum*) are not really a boreal species (they live in the Sierra Nevada of California, and are probably more of a temperate rainforest species. I put them here because they are neat.

Indicator Animal Species

Numerous animal species are found in coniferous forests.

Main Carnivores of the Boreal Forest

Among the main carnivores of the boreal forest are a number of felids (cats) and canids (dogs). The cats range in size from the Siberian Tiger, down through the lynx to the bobcat. The Amur (Siberian) Tigers are but one subspecies of this large Asian cat which is known from the tropics of India and Indonesia all the way north to the boreal forests of Russia.

The Bobcat is a much smaller cat with a range that extends far into the temperate zone, unlike its larger and more northerly relative the lynx.

Herbivores range in size from the large members of the deer family such as the Elk to insects on the small end of the scale.

The name Elk needs some explanation. In Europe, the term Elk is applied to what we in North America would call a moose, and the animal they call a Red Deer is probably in the same species as our Elk. To avoid at least some confusion, a number of authorities in the United States and Canada have begun using a Native American name, Wapiti, in place of the name Elk (of course, scientists use the scientific name *Cervus elaphus* and avoid all confusion).

Among the smaller mammalian herbivores are the arboreal (tree-living) Porcupine and the terrestrial snowshoe hare. The snowshoe hare pictured here is just beginning its winter transformation; the brown coat that camouflaged it so well in the summer and fall is beginning to be shed and replaced with white fur that will help hide it in the winter snows.

The big story in the taiga is adaptation to winter cold and snow. As seen above, the Snowshoe Hare with its large paws (for running over the snow) and white fur (to blend in) is well adapted for life in the snow. Other animals may burrow beneath the snow and forage for their food in tunnels on and in the forest floor; they are insulated from the worst cold of winter by the snow. Still others will hibernate throughout the winter. The cold, however, does take its toll; compared to temperate forests there are fewer species of plants and animals, and among the animals the cold-blooded amphibians and reptiles are noticeably reduced. Bird species mostly deal with the cold by migrating south during the cold winter and returning in the spring. During the brief summer, the very long days that exist at high latitudes means a lot of photosynthesis can take place, and this profusion of plant growth is accompanied by a burst of insect activity. Birds migrating to the taiga in summer are able to take advantage of the new growth and insect abundance - not to mention the reduced competition in the vast forests - and raise their young.

We've already dealt with how the plants deal with the cold in the section on indicator plants, above. One other aspect of the boreal forest with regard to plants should be mentioned, however. The cold, as well as the acid conditions produced by the fallen conifer needles, reduces the rate of decomposition on the forest floor. This in turn reduces the availability of nutrients in the soils, and competition for nutrients by plants growing in the boreal forest may be stiff. In addition, many of the soils are wet and bog-like during the brief summer when the snow finally melts. In many places, the conditions for plants are more reminiscent of a bog. Carnivory, parasitism, use of mycorrhizae – all of these are just a few of the tricks that are used by boreal forest plants.

Perhaps the biggest threat to the boreal forest today is exploration and development of oil and natural gas reserves. From Alaska to Canada to Russia, it is estimated that vast amounts of petroleum products lie under these forests. Increased instability in the Middle East, more effective technology for working in the cold, and the high demand for fossil fuels are pushing exploration and development into areas once thought impossible to exploit. It is not clear whether the slow-growing coniferous forests can recover.

Other threats abound. Perhaps the most serious is Global Warming; as the planet warms the southern reaches of the boreal forest will become warm enough for deciduous trees to outcompete the conifers and replace them. It is not clear whether the tundra areas to the north will support forests even under warmer conditions, and it is less clear if the trees will be able to move north rapidly enough in any event. There is some evidence to suggest that additional carbon dioxide and methane – both greenhouse gasses – will be liberated from warmer tundra and taiga soils as the built up detritus of thousands of years is finally free to decompose. This additional release of greenhouse gasses could accelerate global warming even further.

Logging is always a threat; unless carefully managed these forests are very slow to regrow and corporate pressures may reduce the amount of management and/or accelerate cutting beyond what can be sustained. Large areas of boreal forest have also been flooded as part of hydroelectric projects.

Canids (dogs) are important carnivores in the boreal forest. In North America, the range in size from large (wolves, an expedition is planned for fall 2006 to get pictures of them) to medium (coyotes, see the grassland biome) to small. All of the canids are very adaptable and can be found (or could be found) over a wide range of biomes in North America. Foxes, which prey primarily on small herbivores such as rodents, are well at home in the boreal forests. The red fox is found in Europe, North America, Asia (and has been introduced into Australia) and its range extends from the tundra to the tropics, but the boreal forest seems to be an anchor in its range. The gray fox, on the other hand, is restricted to North America and is more southern in its distribution, only reaching the fringe of the boreal forest (though it may be more common in alpine coniferous forests).

The Porcupine, is well-protected against canid and other predators. Its hindquarters are covered with long barbed quills which penetrate the skin of a predator (particularly near the mouth) and which are difficult to remove once they have attached. The hind view of this porcupine is no accident; with the quills on their backs porcupines quickly turn tail and don't worry too much about close pursuit. They spend much of their time in the trees and feed exclusively on vegetation. Primarily a creature of the north woods, they can also be found in alpine areas, grasslands and even deserts. They do have a few predators, including bobcats and larger members of the weasel family including fishers and wolverines.

The tiny saw-whet owl is sometimes seen in the north woods. In the winter, it may migrate south into temperate forests, but its bread-and-butter hunting grounds are the coniferous forests, including alpine forests in the west. They prefer a forest with at least a few deciduous trees, for these are more likely to harbor boring insects than are the resin-laden conifers. And burrowing insects mean woodpeckers, and woodpeckers mean cavities for the saw-whet owl to nest in. Like most owls, they feed on small mammals such as mice and voles; they may also take small birds, reptiles and amphibians.

The boreal forest and its alpine cousins are host to a wide variety of deer, ranging from the large moose to the whitetail deer. All of these large herbivores prefer the cool forest lest they overheat in the sun, but all need open land on which to graze. Of the deer, moose are perhaps best adapted to wetlands and thrive in the boggy boreal forest. The wapiti prefers mature forest (and more open land in the winter), while the deer move between forest and grassland constantly. In addition to grass and other ground plants, deer of all types can graze on a variety of plant materials including leaves and berries picked from trees overhead; often these are taken by the deer standing on its hind legs. A forest with too many deer may have a 'browse line' where the height of the deer is demonstrated graphically by the absence of green vegetation anywhere in reach of the deer. Such heavy grazing pressure can dramatically alter plant communities. The moose is also a heavy grazer, but compared to the other species it also spends a lot of its time consuming aquatic plants. Mule Deer and White-tailed deer coexist in the western US (the Mule Deer is not found in the east) with the Mule deer preferring open, dry areas to the moister, more covered areas sought out by the smaller white-tails.

Continuing with moose we once again see that these large deer do like to spend time in water. It has seen arguments that one of the reasons they prefer to spend time in water is because of the huge populations of black flies. Black flies, like many insects, are very abundant during the short boreal forest summer, another attraction for the birds that migrate there to raise their young.

This is less of a fire hazard in the boggy, sodden boreal forest than in the well-drained western alpine forests, and indeed wildfires often rage through the latter.

Water plays an important role in the boreal forest (or the alpine forests of the west, for that matter). The Brule River, above, drains a relatively flat boreal forest and the dark brown water carries the stains from the tannins and other plant products produced in the leaves of the species occupying the boggy forest floor. In contrast, the water drains more quickly from the inclined meadows at Tuolumne in Yosemite, where the water runs more clear. Both streams are relatively free of silt and other evidence of soil erosion; both no doubt swell in the spring with snowmelt runoff.

Birches are among the most cold-tolerant of the deciduous trees and their presence is usually a sign that one is at the boundary of a coniferous and a deciduous forest. Aspens play a similar role in the mountains of the western United States.

Northern and southern deer. Reindeer (Caribou in the New World) are the most northern deer species and are relatively large (but not as big as moose or elk). They frequent not only the tundra but the boreal forests as well.

There is a general tendency towards larger body size within a species (or within closely related species) as one moves towards the poles. This apparently has to do with thermoregulation, larger animals are more efficient at retaining body heat in cold climates, while smaller animals can more easily cool off in warmer climates. The rule is known as Bergman's Rule.

CHAPTER

Popular Animals that Live in Rainforests

Many people are familiar with the image of a monkey swinging from a tree or a jaguar prowling on the ground of the rainforests. Animals are a major component of the beauty of rainforests; they provide life and excitement amongst the landscape.

Furthermore, understanding the types of animals that live in the rainforests allows those interested in further study to recognize the importance of the food chain. Although some of the animals may compete for food, living space, or water at times, they all need each other. If one link of the food chain is destroyed, then the entire system of nutrition falls apart.

Insects

From creepy and crawly to colourful and beautiful, insects make up a huge portion of the animal population of rainforests. Most people are familiar with the ants, caterpillars, dragonflies, and moths that inhabit the land. A number of different butterflies are found in the rainforest including the Goliath birdwing, with wing spans up to 11 inches, monarch, gorgeous blue morpho, Queen Alexandra's, with wing spans up to one foot, Saturn, and the swallowtail. Another popular insect is the assassin bug which eats other insects.

Lizards, Reptiles and Amphibians

Crawling through the ground, dangling from the trees, and swimming in the waters are a plethora of alligators, anacondas, caiman crocodiles, emerald tree boas, frogs, iguanas, turtles, red-eyed tree frogs, snakes, toads, and other such creatures. One particularly interesting breed is the chlamydosaurus or the frilled lizard. Circling its head is a seven to 14 inch brightly coloured frill, which it uses to frighten away its enemies.

Birds

Birds soar through the sky in forests, and generally reside in the upper layers of the trees, otherwise known as the canopy. Popular species are the owl, cuckoo, the toucan with its gigantic and colourful beak, the long feathered quetzal, and xenops.

Monkeys and Gorillas

Primates are particularly popular in the rainforests, and one may never even be able to guess how many different types there are roaming through the lands! Of course, there are the well known gorillas, chimpanzees, orangutans, and monkeys. Closely related to the chimpanzee, bonobos are very smart and peaceful creatures that also reside in rainforests. Anyone who sees a siamang, a long-armed, black ape, is very lucky because the species is rather rare.

Other Creatures

Creating a comprehensive categorical list of every animal that lives in the rainforest is difficult, if not impossible, because of the wide varieties of species living in such areas. However, there are still some more animals to be explored.

Perhaps one of the most popular and well known faces of the rainforest is that of the sloth. These furry little creatures spend the majority of their lives hanging upside down from trees, and remain in this position for almost all of their daily activities including sleeping, eating, mating, and giving birth. Tarsiers are almost koala like beings with furry bodies and gigantic eyes, particularly for their small frames.

Large cats, so to speak, such as the jaguar, ocelot, serval, and tiger hunt on the rainforest floor in search of prey. In southeast Asia, the dark, furry binturong can be found searching for fruits and small animals. Bats soar through the air, and piranhas thrash through the waters. Rodents are also present in the rainforests, such as the capybara, the world's largest rodent, mice, and rats.

Examining which animals live in rainforests is both a familiar and new adventure. Many people know that monkeys and jaguars roam through the rainforests; however, some have not even heard of such creatures as the serval and tarsier. Learning about the vast ecosystem of the rainforest is integral to understanding the importance of the environment in general.

Separating the rainforest from the rest of the world is impossible, especially in a time where environmental concerns are on the rise due to problems such as deforestation and global warming. Taking a step back and examining the natural beauty of the rainforests reminds people that these animals' lives are not only important to their own food and life systems, but that they are also beautiful components of the world that are worth fighting for.

The hot, humid conditions which encourage a wide variety of life in the rain forests, change little during the year. Daily variations are greater than seasonal ones. The average temperature is about 27°C, while the rainfall (may be as high as 160 inches) falls regularly - often in heavy thunder-storms.

Animals of the rain forests are provided with a variety of habitats in the different layers of the forest trees. Some live at the top of the tallest trees while others live in the lower zones. Some animals, live on the ground level or even below the surface and so we have this vast and complex pattern of plant and animal life which has been evolving steadily for millions of years.

Sadly, man can all too easily upset the delicate 'balance of nature' and this is already happening in South America and Indonesia where vast areas of forests have been cleared and the plight of already rare species has been made even more precarious. The forests are being cut down to either sell and export the timber or to clear areas due to the demand for more land by an ever increasing population. Two-Toed Sloth (*Choloepus hoffmanni*) - Central & South America. There are two species of two-toed sloth in S. America - Hoffman's (or Unau) found in the forested regions of northern S. America from Ecuador to Costa Rica, and (*Choloepus didattylus*) in Brazil Sloths are slow-moving, tree-dwelling animals that spend almost the whole of their lives hanging upside down from the branches of trees where the growth of algae on their hair provides the excellent greenish camouflage that makes them so difficult to spot. When they are on the ground - perhaps due to a branch breaking - sloths can only move with difficulty.

They eat leaves and fruit. In addition to the two-toed sloths there are three species of three-toed sloth found in the rain forests of South America.

Gorilla (*Gorilla gorilla*) – Central West Africa

Gorillas live in the dense forest of tropical Africa where observation of their daily life becomes extremely difficult. Despite recent successful observations of the mountain gorilla in Zaire, much of their life in the wild remains a mystery.

There are two forms of gorilla. The lowland gorilla and the shaggy-coated mountain gorilla, which was only discovered in 1901

Largest of all the living primates, an adult male will stand five and a half feet tall, with an arm spread of about 8 feet. It will weigh between 400 and 600lb, usually around 450 lb.

Despite its size and great strength, the gorilla is not an aggressive animal and will not usually attack unless its safety, or that of its family, is threatened. Vegetarian in diet, the gorilla leads an orderly family existence, spending much of the day consuming an intake of about 60lb of leaves and fruit!

Giant Anteater or Antbear – Central and South America

In the tropical forests of Central and South America lives the giant anteater or antbear. The antbear can be seven feet in length from its long narrow snout to its bushy tail. It has an extremely long sticky tongue which darts from its snout as it licks up ants or termites, after it has torn open the insects' nest with its powerful curved claws.

Lesser Malay Chevrotain (*Tragus javanicus*) – S. Asia, Sumatra, Java, Borneo

Standing only about 12 inches high at the shoulder, the chevrotain or mouse-deer is one of the smallest of all hoofed animals. Moving on pencil-thin legs, this little animal is a timid forest-dweller, feeding on flowers, fruits, vegetable matter and young leaves.

There are four species in this family; three live in Asia and one in Africa. The males have long upper canine teeth which protrude like fangs below the lips. Neither sex has horns or antlers. In Malay folklore the chevrotain is credited with great cunning (for how else could he evade the many different predators who hunt him?).

Siamang Gibbon (*Hylobates syndactylus*) – Malaya and Sumatra

The siamang is the largest of the seven kinds of gibbon, all of which live in the rain forests of southern Asia. Gibbons are the smallest members of the Ape family and they spend most of their life up in the trees. Their arm over arm movement through the tree tops (known as brachiation) has resulted in the gibbon having very long arms and rather short legs. The saimang stands about three feet tall, but his arm-span may be five feet. Alone among the gibbons, the siamang has a huge vocal sac on the throat which helps him to produce his very loud (and often blood curdling) calls. Food consists of fruit, leaves, insects, young birds and eggs.

Ocelot (*Felis pardalis*) – Central and South America

The ocelot, known in Mexico as the 'tigrillo' or 'little tiger', ranges through the forest regions of Central and South

America from Texas in the north to Brazil and Paraguay in the south. It is the third largest of the South American cats after the jaguar and puma.

A fully grown male measures about four and a half feet from nose to tip of tail. Its beautiful spotted coat provides excellent camouflage in its forest home where it preys on a wide variety of animals, including small deer, agoutis, rats, peccaries, pacas, birds and some reptiles. Sadly, it is much hunted by man for its fur, and it is now seriously threatened. In areas where it is heavily hunted it has become a nocturnal animal, but elsewhere it can be seen in daylight. Although it can climb, the ocelot seems to hunt mainly on the forest floor.

Black Tree Kangaroo (*Dendrolagus ursinus*) – New Guinea

Nine species of tree kangaroo are listed; seven of them live in the dense rain forest of New Guinea, while the other two species inhabit the forests of northern Australia. These animals are about the same size as a wallaby but differ in appearance and have much longer forelimbs and broader feet on the back legs.

Although the tree kangaroo may look rather slow and clumsy on the ground, it can climb quite quickly and with surprising agility. Unlike the majority of kangaroos, tree kangaroos are nocturnal animals, spending the daytime asleep in the trees and then coming down to ground level to spend the night on the forest floor.

Once again, despite their awkward shape for tree-dwelling, these animals can move well in trees and have been known to jump 20 feet from one tree to another. They descend trees tail first. Food consists of leaves and fruit.

Okapi (*Okapia Johnstoni*) – Central Africa

Unknown to science until 1900, when it was discovered by researcher, the Okapi is the only living relative of the giraffe and shares the family name Giraffidae. This large animal has shorter legs than the giraffe and a shorter neck. It stands about 5 ft (approximately 112 metres) at the shoulder and has a sleek purplish coloured coat with black and white bars on the legs. The head is giraffe-like, with a long muzzle, mobile lips and a long tongue for seizing foliage. The horns, which occur only in the males, are capped with a small polished tip which alone protrudes from the skin covering. Okapis live in the densest parts of the rainforest, where they live a solitary existence or move in pairs. They feed on leaves of trees, shrubs and epiphytes. The colouring of the okapi renders it practically invisible even at a short distance.

Common Tree-Shrew (*Tupaia glis*) – S. Asia, Sumatra, Java, Borneo

One of eighteen species of tree-shrew, this remarkable little animal was mistakenly identified as a shrew when it first came to the notice of zoologists. Subsequent investigation proved that this animal was not an insectivore at all, but a very primitive Primate, a member of the family which includes lemurs, monkeys, apes and man! The tree-shrew is a surviving relic from many millions of years ago.

About 14 inches in length, the animal is a skilful climber. Its food consists of a wide variety of plant and animal life.

Orang-Utan (*Pongo Pygmaeus*) – Borneo and Sumatra

Although probably once represented on the mainland of Asia, the orang-utan population of about 5000 is confined to the islands of Borneo and Sumatra. While they are protected on both islands, the steady destruction of their forest territory poses a constant threat to their future.

The orang-utan is the second largest of the apes and the heaviest of all the tree-dwellers It is also the only great ape to be found outside Africa.

Heavily built, with a height of about four and a half feet and a weight of around 200 lb, this ape is normally a rather lethargic mover. It has powerful arms and weak legs, and when on the ground it tends to use the arms as crutches, swinging the body along.

Despite their build and normally lethargic state, the orang-utans are capable of quite rapid movement should the need arise. Seriously threatened, the orang-utan needs full protection if it is going to survive.

Malayan Pangolin (*Manis javanica*) – South-east Asia

Pangolins, or scaly anteaters, are found in tropical Africa, south and south-east Asia.

There are four species in Africa and three in Asia. Although they resemble reptiles, these animals are mammals and their 'scales' are simply mammal hairs, flattened and modified into overlapping plates.

Like the armadillo, the pangolin rolls himself into a tight ball when threatened. The tail is prehensile and it permits the pangolin to hang from the branch of a tree when all four limbs are needed for other purposes such as an attack on a termites nest. Here, the powerful claws rip open the nest while the long sticky tongue mops up the termites. Termites and ants are the chief items of food. Pangolins are completely toothless. Little is known about their ancestry.

Javan Rhinoceros (*Rhinoceros sondaicus*) – S. Asia, Sumatra, Java

All five species of rhinoceros are threatened with extinction. The three Asian species are in great danger, and there are doubts that the rhinoceros can survive in Asia beyond the end of this century.

Like so many other animals, the Javan rhinoceros has suffered heavy persecution at the hand of man, and this once common species declined so rapidly in numbers that in the late 1960's it was thought there were only 24 survivors in the wild.

Thanks to careful conservation and protection the Javan rhinoceros has steadily increased in number over the past few years and in 1991 it was estimated that there might be as many as 60 living in the dense forests of its range. It is the destruction of these forests that will threaten all the successful protection achieved through the efforts of many conservationists from several countries.

The Javan and Gt. Indian rhinoceros have only one horn, the Sumatran rhinoceros has two. The Sumatran is the smallest and hairiest of all the five species.

Slender Loris (*Loris tadirgradus*) – South India and Ceylon

The family Lorisidae includes the slow-moving lorises of Asia, the equally slow angwantibo and potto of Africa, and the anything but slow-moving galagos or bushbabies found in southern and eastern Africa.

The slender loris lives in the jungles of southern India and Ceylon. It is a lightly built creature with long, spindly legs, slender body and large brilliant eyes. At one time the eyes of the slender loris were used as an ingredient of love potions!

It is a nocturnal animal, sleeping through the day and waking at sunset to move stealthily through the trees in search of its diet of insects, small birds, lizards and fruit.

Malayan Tapir (*Tapirus indicus*) – Malaysia

Tapir is the name given to the four surviving species of this large woodland mammal which form the family Tapiridae of the order Perissodactyla (odd-toed hooved animals). They are heavily built creatures with four front and three hind toes, a practically non-existent tail and with the nose and upper-lip forming a short flexible trunk.

Three of the four species live in Central and South America, but the fourth is to be found in the rainforests of Malaysia. The Malayan Tapir is easily recognised by his black and white colouring. This animal may stand 3 and a half feet (approximately 1 metre) at the shoulder. It is shy, nocturnal and quite inoffensive, frequenting deep forests and keeping close to water and mud. Its diet is exclusively vegetarian. The young are spotted and striped with white.

Jaguar (*Panthera onca*) – Central and South America

This is the largest of the New World cats, a fully grown male measuring up to 8ft from nose to tip of tail. It is a heavier animal than the leopards of Africa and Asia although similar in size. The jaguar differs from the leopard in having a more powerful head, shorter tail and shout stout legs. It is found on the edges of forests and often beside rivers from the southern United States to northern Argentina. Unlike most cats it seems to like water and obviously enjoys swimming. It will even fish with its paws. The diet of the jaguar includes capybaras, peccaries, deer, agoutis, tapir and fish. Heavily hunted by man for its skin, the jaguar is steadily declining in numbers - and the destruction of the rain forests will speed this decline considerably.

Snakes

Snakes, like all reptiles, are cold-blooded animals which cannot adjust their body temperature internally. The constant warmth and humidity of tropical rain forests provide an ideal habitat where snakes can live without having to shelter from heat or cold.

Snakes of the rain forest are well adapted to an arboreal or tree-dwelling existence. Many have long thin bodies with angled scales on their bellies which help the snakes to grip branches. Other species have developed 'wings', enabling the snake to escape predators by gliding to another tree or the ground. Ground-dwelling snakes track by scent but in the trees the scent trail is broken whenever the prey crosses to another branch, so many tree-living species hunt by sight. Some have prehensile tails which can grip a branch firmly while the rest of the body moves on. Snakes are well camouflaged; the most common colours are green or brown to match leaves or bark, often with a twig-like or leaf-like pattern.

Boas

Like the pythons of Africa and Asia the boas of South America kill by constriction. The largest boa is the anaconda, which averages 35ft in length and hunts along river banks. Other boas include the boa constrictor and the emerald tree boa.

Pythons

Pythons include many species of non-poisonous snakes which kill their prey, such as birds and small mammals, by constriction. The snake coils its long body round its victim and squeezes it to death. The largest python is the reticulated python of Asia; it can grow to 33 ft long and weigh 300 lb. The 3 ft long burrowing python of Africa is the smallest python.

Venomous Species

Poisonous snakes use their venom mainly for feeding rather than for defence. There are three main groups:

Rear-Fanged Snakes

The snakes in this group have the two or three rearmost teeth of the upper jaw enlarged and grooved for injecting venom. Few species are very poisonous and only two, both African tree snakes, are dangerous to man

Front Fixed-Fang Snakes

The fangs of these snakes are fixed at the front of the upper jaw. This group includes many deadly species, such as the mambas of Africa, the cobras of Africa and Asia, and the coral snakes of the New World.

Folding Fang Snakes

These snakes have a large pair of poison fangs at the front of the upper jaw. The fangs lie flat when not needed and are raised when the snake strikes. The group consists of the vipers and pit-vipers, for example the rattlesnakes and the bushmaster snake of Central and South America.

CHAPTER

7

The Biodiversity of the Rainforests

Why should the loss of tropical forests be of any concern to us in light of our own poor management of natural resources? The loss of tropical rainforests has a profound and devastating impact on the world because rainforests are so biologically diverse, more so than other ecosystems (e.g., temperate forests) on Earth.

Consider these facts:

- A single pond in Brazil can sustain a greater variety of fish than is found in all of Europe's rivers.
- A 25-acre plot of rainforest in Borneo may contain more than 700 species of trees - a number equal to the total tree diversity of North America.
- A single rainforest reserve in Peru is home to more species of birds than are found in the entire United States.
- One single tree in Peru was found to harbor forty-three different species of ants - a total that approximates the entire number of ant species in the British Isles.
- The number of species of fish in the Amazon exceeds the number found in the entire Atlantic Ocean.

The biodiversity of the tropical rainforest is so immense that less than 1 per cent of its millions of species have been studied by scientists for their active constituents and their possible uses. When an acre of topical rainforest is lost, the impact on the number of plant and animal species lost and their possible uses is staggering. Scientists estimate that we are losing more than 137 species of plants and animals every single day because of rainforest deforestation.

Surprisingly, scientists have a better understanding of how many stars there are in the galaxy than they have of how many species there are on Earth. Estimates vary from 2 million to 100 million species, with a best estimate of somewhere near 10 million; only 1.4 million of these species have actually been named. Today, rainforests occupy only 2 per cent of the entire Earth's surface and 6 per cent of the world's land surface, yet these remaining lush rainforests support over half of our planet's wild plants and trees and one-half of the world's wildlife. Hundreds and thousands of these rainforest species are being extinguished before they have even been identified, much less catalogued and studied. The magnitude of this loss to the world was most poignantly described by researcher Prize-winning biologist over a decade ago:

> "The worst thing that can happen during the 1980s is not energy depletion, economic collapses, limited nuclear war, or conquest by a totalitarian government. As terrible as these catastrophes would be for us, they can be repaired within a few generations. The one process ongoing in the 1980s that will take millions of years to correct is the loss of genetic and species diversity by the destruction of natural habitats. This is the folly that our descendants are least likely to forgive us for".

Yet still the destruction continues. If deforestation continues at current rates, scientists estimate nearly 80 to 90 per cent of tropical rainforest ecosystems will be destroyed by the year 2020. This destruction is the main force driving a species extinction rate unmatched in 65 million years.

The Disappearing Rainforests

- We are losing Earth's greatest biological treasures just as we are beginning to appreciate their true value. Rainforests once covered 14 per cent of the earth's land surface; now they cover a mere 6 per cent and experts estimate that the last remaining rainforests could be consumed in less than 40 years.

- One and one-half acres of rainforest are lost every second with tragic consequences for both developing and industrial countries.
- Rainforests are being destroyed because the value of rainforest land is perceived as only the value of its timber by short-sighted governments, multi-national logging companies, and land owners.
- Nearly half of the world's species of plants, animals and microorganisms will be destroyed or severely threatened over the next quarter century due to rainforest deforestation.
- Experts estimates that we are losing 137 plant, animal and insect species every single day due to rainforest deforestation. That equates to 50,000 species a year. As the rainforest species disappear, so do many possible cures for life-threatening diseases. Currently, 121 prescription drugs sold worldwide come from plant-derived sources. While 25 per cent of Western pharmaceuticals are derived from rainforest ingredients, less that 1 per cent of these tropical trees and plants have been tested by scientists.
- Most rainforests are cleared by chainsaws, bulldozers and fires for its timber value and then are followed by farming and ranching operations, even by world giants like Mitsubishi Corporation, Georgia Pacific, Texaco and Unocal.
- There were an estimated ten million Indians living in the Amazonian Rainforest five centuries ago. Today there are less than 200,000.
- In Brazil alone, European colonists have destroyed more than 90 indigenous tribes since the 1900's. With them have gone centuries of accumulated knowledge of the medicinal value of rainforest species. As their homelands continue to be destroyed by deforestation, rainforest peoples are also disappearing.

- Most medicine men and shamans remaining in the Rainforests today are 70 years old or more. Each time a rainforest medicine man dies, it is as if a library has burned down.
- When a medicine man dies without passing his arts on to the next generation, the tribe and the world loses thousands of years of irreplaceable knowledge about medicinal plants.

The Wealth of the Rainforests

- The Amazon Rainforest covers over a billion acres, encompassing areas in Brazil, Venezuela, Colombia and the Eastern Andean region of Ecuador and Peru. If Amazonia were a country, it would be the ninth largest in the world.
- The Amazon Rainforest has been described as the 'Lungs of our Planet' because it provides the essential environmental world service of continuously recycling carbon dioxide into oxygen. More than 20 per cent of the world oxygen is produced in the Amazon Rainforest.
- More than half of the world's estimated 10 million species of plants, animals and insects live in the tropical rainforests. One-fifth of the world's fresh water is in the Amazon Basin.
- One hectare (2.47 acres) may contain over 750 types of trees and 1500 species of higher plants.
- At least 80 per cent of the developed world's diet originated in the tropical rainforest. Its bountiful gifts to the world include fruits like avocados, coconuts, figs, oranges, lemons, grapefruit, bananas, guavas, pineapples, mangos and tomatoes; vegetables including corn, potatoes, rice, winter squash and yams; spices like black pepper, cayenne, chocolate, cinnamon, cloves, ginger, sugar cane, tumeric, coffee and vanilla and nuts including Brazil nuts and cashews.
- At least 3000 fruits are found in the rainforests; of these only 200 are now in use in the Western World. The Indians of the rainforest use over 2000.

- Rainforest plants are rich in secondary metabolites, particularly alkaloids. Biochemists believe alkaloids protect plants from disease and insect attacks. Many alkaloids from higher plants have proven to be of medicinal value and benefit.
- Currently, 121 prescription drugs currently sold worldwide come from plant-derived sources. And while 25 per cent of Western pharmaceuticals are derived from rainforest ingredients, less than 1 per cent of these tropical trees and plants have been tested by scientists.
- The U.S. National Cancer Institute has identified 3000 plants that are active against cancer cells. 70 per cent of these plants are found in the rainforest. Twenty-five per cent of the active ingredients in today's cancer-fighting drugs come from organisms found only in the rainforest.
- Vincristine, extracted from the rainforest plant, periwinkle, is one of the world's most powerful anticancer drugs. It has dramatically increased the survival rate for acute childhood leukemia since its discovery.
- In 1983, there were no U.S. pharmaceutical manufacturers involved in research programmes to discover new drugs or cures from plants. Today, over 100 pharmaceutical companies and several branches of the US government, including giants like Merck and The National Cancer Institute, are engaged in plant research projects for possible drugs and cures for viruses, infections, cancer, and even AIDS.

Rainforest Action

- Experts agree that by leaving the rainforests intact and harvesting it's many nuts, fruits, oil-producing plants, and medicinal plants, the rainforest has more economic value than if they were cut down to make grazing land for cattle or for timber.
- The latest statistics show that rainforest land converted to cattle operations yields the land owner $60 per acre and if timber is harvested, the land is worth $400 per

acre. However, if these renewable and sustainable resources are harvested, the land will yield the land owner $2,400 per acre.

- If managed properly, the rainforest can provide the world's need for these natural resources on a perpetual basis.
- Promoting the use of these sustainable and renewable sources could stop the destruction of the rainforests. By creating a new source of income harvesting the medicinal plants, fruits nuts, oil and other sustainable resources, the rainforests is be more valuable alive than cut and burned.
- Sufficient demand of sustainable and ecologically harvested rainforest products is necessary for preservation efforts to succeed. Purchasing sustainable rainforest products can effect positive change by creating a market for these products while supporting the native people's economy and provides the economic solution and alternative to cutting the forest just for the value of its timber.

The Importance of Rain Forest

The beauty, majesty, and timelessness of a primary rainforest are indescribable. It is impossible to capture on film, to describe in words, or to explain to those who have never had the awe-inspiring experience of standing in the heart of a primary rainforest.

Rainforests have evolved over millions of years to turn into the incredibly complex environments they are today. Rainforests represent a store of living and breathing renewable natural resources that for eons, by virtue of their richness in both animal and plant species, have contributed a wealth of resources for the survival and well-being of humankind. These resources have included basic food supplies, clothing, shelter, fuel, spices, industrial raw materials, and medicine for all those who have lived in the majesty of the forest. However, the inner dynamics of a tropical rainforest is an intricate and fragile system. Everything is so interdependent that upsetting one part can lead to unknown damage or even destruction of the whole. Sadly, it has taken only a century of human intervention to destroy what nature designed to last forever.

The scale of human pressures on ecosystems everywhere has increased enormously in the last few decades. Since 1980 the global economy has tripled in size and the world population has increased by 30 per cent. Consumption of everything on the planet has risen- at a cost to our ecosystems. In 2001, The World Resources Institute estimated that the demand for rice, wheat, and corn is expected to grow by 40 per cent by 2020, increasing irrigation water demands by 50 per cent or more. They further reported that the demand for wood could double by the year 2050; unfortunately, it is still the tropical forests of the world that supply the bulk of the world's demand for wood.

In 1950, about 15 per cent of the Earth's land surface was covered by rainforest. Today, more than half has already gone up in smoke. In fewer than fifty years, more than half of the world's tropical rainforests have fallen victim to fire and the chain saw, and the rate of destruction is still accelerating. Unbelievably, more than 200,000 acres of rainforest are burned every day. That is more than 150 acres lost every minute of every day, and 78 million acres lost every year! More than 20 per cent of the Amazon rainforest is already gone, and much more is severely threatened as the destruction continues. It is estimated that the Amazon alone is vanishing at a rate of 20,000 square miles a year. If nothing is done to curb this trend, the entire Amazon could well be gone within fifty years.

Massive deforestation brings with it many ugly consequences-air and water pollution, soil erosion, malaria epidemics, the release of carbon dioxide into the atmosphere, the eviction and decimation of indigenous Indian tribes, and the loss of biodiversity through extinction of plants and animals. Fewer rainforests mean less rain, less oxygen for us to breathe, and an increased threat from global warming.

But who is really to blame? Consider what we industrialized Americans have done to our own homeland. We converted 90 per cent of North America's virgin forests into firewood, shingles, furniture, railroad ties, and paper. Other industrialized countries have done no better. Malaysia, Indonesia, Brazil, and other tropical countries with rainforests are often branded as 'environmental villains' of the world, mainly because of their reported levels of destruction of their rainforests. But despite the levels of deforestation, up to 60 per cent of their territory is still covered by natural tropical forests. In fact, today, much of the pressures on their remaining rainforests comes from servicing the needs and markets for wood products in industrialized countries that have already depleted their own natural resources. Industrial countries would not be buying rainforest hardwoods and timber had we not cut down our own trees long ago, nor would poachers in the Amazon jungle be slaughtering jaguar, ocelot, caiman, and otter if we did not provide lucrative markets for their skins in Berlin, Paris, and Tokyo.

The Amazon Rain Forest

If Amazonia were a country, it would be the ninth largest in the world. The Amazon rainforest, the world's greatest remaining natural resource, is the most powerful and bioactively diverse natural phenomenon on the planet. It has been described as the 'lungs of our planet' because it provides the essential service of continuously recycling carbon dioxide into oxygen. It is estimated that more than 20 per cent of Earth's oxygen is produced in this area.

The Amazon covers more than 1.2 billion acres, representing two-fifths of the enormous South American continent, and is found in nine South American countries: Brazil, Colombia, Peru, Venezuela, Ecuador, Bolivia, Guyana, French Guiana, and Suriname. With 2.5 million square miles of rainforest, the Amazon rainforest represents 54 per cent of the total rainforests left on Earth.

The Amazon River

The life force of the Amazon rainforest is the mighty Amazon River. It starts as a trickle high in the snow-capped Andes Mountains and flows more than 4,000 miles across the South American continent until it enters the Atlantic Ocean at Belem, Brazil, where it is 200 to 300 miles across, depending on the season. Even 1,000 miles inland it is still 7 miles wide. The river is so deep that ocean liners can travel up its length to 2,300 miles inland. The Amazon River flows through the center of the rainforest and is fed by 1,100 tributaries, 17 of which are more than 1,000 miles long. The Amazon is by far the largest watershed and largest river system in the world occupying over 6 million square kilometres. Over two-thirds of all the fresh water found on Earth is in the Amazon Basin's rivers, streams, and tributaries.

With so much water it's not unusual that the main mode of transportation throughout the area is by boat. The smallest and most common boats used today are still made out of hollowed tree trunks, whether they are powered by outboard motors or more often by human-powered paddles. Almost 14,000 miles of Amazon waterway are navigable, and several million miles through swamps and forests are penetrable by canoe. The enormous Amazon River carries massive amounts of silt from runoff from the rainforest floor. Massive amounts of silt deposited at the mouth of the Amazon River has created the largest river island in the world-Marajo Island, which is roughly the size of Switzerland. With this massive freshwater system, it is not unusual that life beneath the water is as abundant and diverse as the surrounding rainforest's plant and animal species. More than 2,000 species of fish have been identified in the Amazon Basin - more species than in the entire Atlantic Ocean.

Largest Collection of Plant and Animal Species

The Amazon Basin was formed in the Paleozoic period, somewhere between 500 million and 200 million years ago. The extreme age of the region in geologic terms has much to do with the relative infertility of the rainforest soil and the richness and unique diversity of the plant and animal life. There are more fertile areas in the Amazon River's flood plain, where the river deposits richer soil brought from the Andes, which only formed 20 million years ago.

The Amazon rainforest contains the largest collection of living plant and animal species in the world. The diversity of plant species in the Amazon rainforest is the highest on Earth. It is estimated that a single hectare (2.47 acres) of Amazon rainforest contains about 900 tons of living plants, including more than 750 types of trees and 1500 other plants. The Andean mountain range and the Amazon jungle are home to more than half of the world's species of flora and fauna; in fact, one in five of all the birds in the world live in the rainforests of the Amazon. To date, some 438,000 species of plants of economic and social interest have been registered in the region, and many more have yet to be catalogued or even discovered.

Scarring and Loss of Diversity

Once a vast sea of tropical forest, the Amazon rainforest today is scarred by roads, farms, ranches, and dams. Brazil is gifted with a full third of the world's remaining rainforests; unfortunately, it is also one of the world's great rainforest destroyers, burning or felling more than 2.7 million acres each year. More than 20 per cent of rainforest in the Amazon has been razed and is gone forever. This ocean of green, nearly as large as Australia, is the last great rainforest in the known universe and it is being decimated like the others before it. Why? Like other rainforests already lost forever, the land is being cleared for logging timber, large-scale cattle ranching, mining operations, government road building and hydroelectric schemes, military operations, and the subsistence agriculture of peasants and landless settlers. Sadder still, in many places the rainforests are burnt simply to provide charcoal to power industrial plants in the area.

Driving Forces of Destruction

Commercial logging is the single largest cause of rainforest destruction, both directly and indirectly. Other activities destroying the rainforest, including clearing land for grazing animals and subsistence farming. The simple fact is that people are destroying the Amazon rainforest and the rest of the rainforests of the world because 'they can't see the forest for the trees'.

Logging for Tropical Hardwoods

Logging tropical hardwoods like teak, mahogany, rosewood, and other timber for furniture, building materials, charcoal, and other wood products is big business and big profits. Several species of tropical hardwoods are imported by developed counties, including the United States, just to build coffins that are then buried or burned. The demand, extraction, and consumption of tropical hardwoods has been so massive that some countries that have been traditional exporters of tropical hardwoods are now importing them because they have already exhausted their supply by destroying their native rainforests in slash-and-burn operations. It is anticipated that the Philippines, Malaysia, the Ivory Coast, Nigeria, and Thailand will soon follow, as all these countries will run out of rainforest hardwood timber for export within five years. Japan is the largest importer of tropical woods. Despite recent reductions, Japan's average tropical timber import of 11 million cubic metres annually is still gluttonous. The demand for tropical hardwood timber is damaging to the ecological, biological, and social fabric of tropical lands and is clearly unsustainable for any length of time.

Behind the hardwood logger come others down the same roads built to transport the timber. The cardboard packing and the wood chipboard industries use 15-ton machines that gobble up the rainforest with 8-foot cutting discs that have eight blades revolving 320 times a minute. These machines that cut entire trees into chips half the size of a matchbox can gobble up more than 200 species of trees in mere minutes.

Logging rainforest timber is a large economic source, and in many cases, the main source of revenue for servicing the national debt of these developing countries. Logging profits are real to these countries that must service their debts, but they are fleeting. Governments are selling their assets too cheaply, and once the rainforest is gone, their source of income will also be gone. Sadly, most of the real profits of the timber trade are made not by the developing countries, but by multinational companies and industrialists of the Northern Hemisphere. These huge, profit-driven logging companies pay governments a fraction of the timber's worth for large logging concessions on immense tracts of rainforest land and reap huge profits by harvesting the timber in the most economical manner feasible with little regard to the destruction left in their wake.

Logging concessions in the Amazon are sold for as little as $2 per acre, with logging companies felling timber worth thousands of dollars per acre. Governments are selling their natural resources, hawking for pennies resources that soon will be worth billions of dollars. Some of these government concessions and land deals made with industrialists make the sale of Manhattan for $24 worth of trinkets look shrewd. In 1986 a huge industrial timber corporation bought thousands of acres in the Borneo rainforest by giving 2,000 Malaysian dollars to twelve longhouses of local tribes. This sum amounted to the price of two bottles of beer for each member of the community. Since then, this company and others have managed to extract and destroy about a third of the Borneo rainforest - about 6.9 million acres - and the local tribes have been evicted from the area or forced to work for the logging companies at slave wages.

Fuel Wood and the Paper Industry

In addition to being logged for exportation, rainforest wood stays in developing countries for fuel wood and charcoal. One single steel plant in Brazil making steel for Japanese cars needs millions of tons of wood each year to produce charcoal that can be used in the manufacture of steel. Then, there is the paper industry.

One pulpwood project in the Brazilian Amazon consists of a Japanese power plant and pulp mill. To set up this single plant operation, 5,600 square miles of Amazon rainforest were burned to the ground and replanted with pulpwood trees. This single manufacturing plant consumes 2,000 tons of surrounding rainforest wood every day to produce 55 megawatts of electricity to run the plant. The plant, which has been in operation since 1978, produces more than 750 tons of pulp for paper every 24 hours, worth approximately $500,000, and has built 2,800 miles of roads through the Amazon rainforest to be used by its 700 vehicles. In addition to this pulp mill, the world's biggest pulp mill is the Aracruz mill in Brazil. Its two units produce 1 million tons of pulp a year, harvesting the rainforest to keep the plant in business and displacing thousands of indigenous tribes. Where does all this pulp go? Aracruz's biggest customers are the United States, Belgium, Great Britain, and Japan. More and more rainforest is destroyed to meet the demands of the developed world's paper industry, which requires a staggering 200 million tons of wood each year simply to make paper. If the present rate continues, it is estimated that the paper industry alone will consume 4 billion tons of wood annually by the year 2020.

Once an area of rainforest has been logged, even if it is given the rare chance to regrow, it can never become what it once was. The intricate ecosystem nature devised is lost forever. Only 1 to 2 per cent of light at the top of a rainforest canopy manages to reach the forest floor below. Most times when timber is harvested, trees and other plants that have evolved over centuries to grow in the dark, humid environment below the canopy simply cannot live out in the open, and as a result, the plants and animals (that depend on the plants) of the original forest become extinct Even if only sections of land throughout an area are destroyed, these remnants change drastically. Birds and other animals cannot cross from one remnant of land to another in the canopy, so plants are not pollinated, seeds are not dispersed by the animals, and the plants around the edges are not surrounded by the high jungle humidity they need to grow properly. As a result, the remnants slowly become degraded and die. Rains come and wash away the thin topsoil that was previously protected by the canopy, and this barren, infertile land is vulnerable to erosion. Sometimes the land is replanted in African grasses for cattle operations; other times more virgin rainforest is destroyed for cattle operations because grass planted on recently burned land has a better chance to grow.

The Grazing Land

As the demand in the Western world for cheap meat increases, more and more rainforests are destroyed to provide grazing land for animals. In Brazil alone, there are an estimated 220 million head of cattle, 20 million goats, 60 million pigs, and 700 million chickens. Most of Central and Latin America's tropical and temperate rainforests have been lost to cattle operations to meet the world demand, and still the cattle operations continue to move southward into the heart of the South American rainforests. To graze one steer in Amazonia takes two full acres. Most of the ranchers in the Amazon operate at a loss, yielding only paper profits purely as tax shelters. Ranchers' fortunes are made only when ranching is supported by government giveaways. A banker or rich landowner in Brazil can slash and burn a huge tract of land in the Amazon rainforest, seed it with grass for cattle, and realize millions of dollars worth of government-subsidized loans, tax credits, and write-offs in return for developing the land. These government development schemes rarely make a profit, as they are actually selling cheap beef to industrialized nations. One single cattle operation in Brazil that was co-owned by British Barclays Bank and one of Brazil's wealthiest families was responsible for the destruction of almost 500,000 acres of virgin rainforest. The cattle operation never made a profit, but government write-offs sheltered huge logging profits earned off of logging other land in the Brazilian rainforest owned by the same investors. These generous tax and credit incentives have created more than 29 million acres of large cattle ranches in the Brazilian Amazon, even though the typical ranch could cover less than half its costs without these subsidies. Even these grazing lands don't last forever. Soon the lack of nutrients in the soil and overgrazing degrade them, and they are abandoned for newly cleared land. In Brazil alone, more than 63,000 square miles of land has reportedly been abandoned in this way.

Subsistence Farming

This type of government-driven destruction of rainforest land is promoted by a common attitude among governments in rainforest regions, an attitude that the forest is an economic resource to be harnessed to aid in the development of their countries. The same attitudes that accompanied the colonization of our own frontier are found today in Brazil and other countries with wild and unharnessed rainforest wilderness. These beliefs are exemplified by one Brazilian official's public statement that "not until all Amazonas is colonized by real Brazilians, not Indians, can we truly say we own it." Were we Americans any different with our own colonization, decimating the North American Indian tribes? Like Brazil, we sent out a call to all the world that America had land for the landless in an effort to increase colonization of our country at the expense of our indigenous Indian tribes. And like the first American colonists, colonization in the rainforest really means subsistence farming.

Subsistence farming has for centuries been a driving force in the loss of rainforest land. And as populations explode in Third-World countries in South America and the Far East, the impact has been profound. By tradition, wildlands and unsettled lands in the rainforest are free to those who clear the forest and till the soil. 'Squatter's rights' still prevail, and poor, hungry people show little enthusiasm for arguments about the value of biodiversity or the plight of endangered species when they struggle daily to feed their families. These landless peasants and settlers follow the logging companies down the roads they've built to extract timber into untouched rainforest lands, burning off whatever the logging companies left behind.

The present approach to rainforest cultivation produces wealth for a few, but only for a short time, because farming burned-off tracts of Amazon rainforest seldom works for long. Less than 10 per cent of Amazonian soils are suitable for sustained conventional agriculture. However lush they look, rainforests often flourish on such nutrient-poor soils that they are essentially 'wet deserts', easier to damage and harder to cultivate than any other soil. Most are exhausted by the time they have produced three or four crops. Many of the thousands of homesteaders who migrated from Brazil's cities to the wilds of the rainforest, responding to the government's call of 'land without men for men without land', have already had to abandon their depleted farms and move on, leaving behind fields of baked clay dotted with stagnant pools of polluted water. Experts agree that the path to conservation begins with helping these local residents meet their own daily needs. Because of the infertility of the soil, and the lack of knowledge of sustainable cultivation practices, this type of agriculture strips the soil of nutrients within a few harvests, and the farmers continue to move farther into the rainforest in search of new land. They must be helped and educated to break free of the need to continually clear rainforest in search of fresh, fertile land if the rainforest is to be saved.

Leading the Threat: Governments

Directly and indirectly, the leading threats to rainforest ecosystems are governments and their unbridled, unplanned, and uncoordinated development of natural resources. The 2000-2001 World Resources Report put out by the United Nations reported that governments worldwide spend $700 billion dollars a year supporting and subsidizing environmentally unsound practices in the use of water, agriculture, energy, and transportation. In the Amazon, rainforest timber exports and large-scale development projects go a long way in servicing national debt in many developing countries, which is why governments and international aid-lending institutions like the World Bank subsidize them. In the tropics, governments own or control nearly 80 per cent of tropical forests, so these forests stand or fall according to government policy; and in many countries, government policies lie behind the wastage of forest resources. Besides the tax incentives and credit subsidies that guarantee large profits to private investors who convert forests to pastures and farms, governments allow private concessionaires to log the national forests on terms that induce uneconomic or wasteful uses of the public domain. Massive public expenditures on highways, dams, plantations, and agricultural settlements, too often supported by multilateral development lending, convert or destroy large areas of forest for projects of questionable economic worth.

Tropical countries are among the poorest countries on Earth. Brazil alone spends 40 per cent of its annual income simply servicing its loans, and the per capita income of Brazil's people is less than $2,000 annually. Sadly, these numbers don't even represent an accurate picture in the Amazon because Brazil is one of the richer countries in South America. These struggling Amazonian countries must also manage the most complex, delicate, and valuable forests remaining on the planet, and the economic and technological resources available to them are limited. They must also endure a dramatic social and economic situation, as well as deeply adverse terms of trade and financial relationships with industrial countries. Under such conditions, the possibility of their reaching sustainable models of development alone is virtually nil.

There is a clear need for industrial countries to sincerely and effectively assist the tropics in a quest for sustainable forest management and development if the remaining rainforests are to be saved. The governments of these developing countries need help in learning how to manage and protect their natural resources for long-term profits, while still managing to service their debts, and they must be given the incentives and tools to do so. Programmes to redefine the timber concessions so concessionaires have greater incentives to guard the long-term health of the forest and programmes to revive and expand community-based forestry schemes, which ensure more rational use of forests and a better life for the people who live near them, must be developed.

First-World capital must seek out opportunities to partner with organisations that have the technical expertise to guide these programmes of sustainable economic development. In addition, programmes teaching techniques for sustainable harvesting practices and identifying profitable, yet sustainable, forest products can enable developing countries to improve the standard of living for their people, service national debt, and contribute meaningfully to land use planning and conservation of natural resources.

Rainforests Pharmacy to the World

It is estimated that nearly half of the world's estimated 10 million species of plants, animals, and microorganisms will be destroyed or severely threatened over the next quarter-century due to rainforest deforestation. Edward O. Wilson estimates that we are losing 137 plant and animal species every single day. That's 50,000 species a year! Again, why should we in the United States be concerned about the destruction of distant tropical rainforests? Because rainforest plants are complex chemical storehouses that contain many undiscovered biodynamic compounds with unrealized potential for use in modern medicine. We can gain access to these materials only if we study and conserve the species that contain them.

Rainforests currently provide sources for one-fourth of today's medicines, and 70 per cent of the plants found to have anticancer properties are found only in the rainforest. The rainforest and its immense undiscovered biodiversity hold the key to unlocking tomorrow's cures for devastating diseases. How many cures for devastating disease have we already lost?

Two drugs obtained from a rainforest plant known as the Madagascar periwinkle, now extinct in the wild due to deforestation of the Madagascar rainforest, have increased the chances of survival for children with leukemia from 20 per cent to 80 per cent. Think about it: eight out of ten children are now saved, rather than eight of ten children dying from leukemia. How many children have been spared and how many more will continue to be spared because of this single rainforest plant? What if we had failed to discover this one important plant among millions before human activities had led to its extinction? When our remaining rainforests are gone, the rare plants and animals will be lost forever-and so will the possible cures for diseases like cancer they can provide.

No one can challenge the fact that we are still largely dependent on plants for treating our ailments. Almost 90 per cent of people in developing countries still rely on traditional medicine, based largely on different species of plants and animals, for their primary health care. In the United States, some 25 per cent of prescriptions are filled with drugs whose active ingredients are extracted or derived from plants. By 1980 sales of these plant-based drugs in the United States amounted to some $4.5 billion annually. Worldwide sales of these plant-based drugs were estimated at $40 billion in 1990. Currently 121 prescription drugs sold worldwide come from plant-derived sources from only 90 species of plants. Still more drugs are derived from animals and microorganisms.

More than 25 per cent of the active ingredients in today's cancer-fighting drugs come from organisms found only in the rainforest. The U.S. National Cancer Institute has identified more than 3,000 plants that are active against cancer cells, and 70 per cent of these plants are found only in the rainforest. In the thousands of species of rainforest plants that have not been analyzed are many more thousands of unknown plant chemicals, many of which have evolved to protect the plants from diseases. These plant chemicals may well help us in our own ongoing struggle with constantly evolving pathogens, including bacteria, viruses, and fungi that are mutating against our mainstream drugs and becoming resistant to them. These pathogens cause serious diseases, including hepatitis, pneumonia, tuberculosis, and HIV, all of which are becoming more difficult to treat. Experts now believe that if there is a cure for cancer and even AIDS, it will probably be found in the rainforest.

Bioprospecting

In 1983, there were no U.S. pharmaceutical manufacturers involved in research programmes to discover new drugs or cures from plants. Today, more than 100 pharmaceutical companies, including giants like Merck, Abbott, Bristol-Myers Squibb, Eli Lilly, Monsanto, Smith-Kline Beecham, as well as several branches of the U.S. government, including the National Cancer Institute, are engaged in plant-based research projects trying to find possible drugs to treat infections, cancer, and AIDS. Most of this research is currently taking place in the rainforest in an industry that is now called 'bioprospecting'. This new pharmacological industry draws together an unlikely confederacy: plant collectors and anthropologists; ecologists and conservationists; natural product companies and nutritional supplement manufacturers; AIDS and cancer researchers; executives in the world's largest drug companies; and native indigenous shamans. They are part of a radical experiment: to preserve the world's rainforests by showing how much more valuable they are standing than cut down. And it is a race against a clock whose every tick means another acre of charred forest. Yet, it is also a race that pits one explorer against another, for those who score the first big hit in chemical bioprospecting will secure wealth and a piece of scientific immortality.

In November 1991, Merck Pharmaceutical Company announced a landmark agreement to obtain samples of wild plants and animals for drug-screening purposes from Costa Rica's National Biodiversity Institute (INBio); the programme is still ongoing today. Spurred by this and other biodiversity prospecting ventures, interest in the commercial value of plant genetic and biochemical resources is burgeoning today. While the Merck-INBio agreement provides a fascinating example of a private partnership that contributes to rural economic development, rainforest conservation, and technology transfer, virtually no precedent exists for national policies and legislation to govern and regulate what amounts to a brand new industry.

Since wealth and technology are as concentrated in most of the North as biodiversity and poverty are in much of the South, the question of equity is particularly hard to answer in ways that satisfy everyone with a stake in the outcome. The interests of bioprospecting corporations are not the same as those of people who live in a biodiversity "hot spot," many of them barely eking out a living. As the search for wild species whose genes can yield new medicines and better crops gathers momentum, these rich habitats also sport more and more bioprospectors. Like the nineteenth-century California gold rush or its present-day counterpart in Brazil, this 'gene rush' could wreak havoc on ecosystems and the people living in or near them. Done properly, however, bioprospecting can bolster both economic and conservation goals while underpinning the medical and agricultural advances needed to combat disease and sustain growing populations.

The majority of our current plant-derived drugs were discovered by examining the traditional use of plants by the indigenous people who lived where the plants grew and flourished. History has shown that the situation with the rainforest is no different, and bioprospectors now are working side by side with rainforest tribal shamans and herbal healers to learn the wealth of their plant knowledge and about the many uses of indigenous plants.

The Secrets of Rainforests

After the Amerindians discovered America, about twenty millennia before Columbus, all their clothing, food, medicine, and shelter were derived from the forests. Those millennia gave the Indians time to discover and learn empirically the virtues and vices of the thousands of edible and medicinal species in the rainforest. More than 80 per cent of the developed world's diet originated in the rainforest and from this empirical indigenous knowledge of the wealth of edible fruits, vegetables, and nuts. Of the estimated 3,000 edible fruits found in the rainforest, only 200 are cultivated for use today, despite the fact that the Indians used more than 1,500. Many secrets and untold treasures about the medicinal plants used by shamans, healers, and the indigenous people of the rainforest tribes await discovery. Long regarded as hocus-pocus by science, the empirical plant knowledge of the indigenous peoples is now thought by many to be the Amazon's new gold. Their use of the plants provides the bioprospector with the clues necessary to target specific species to research in the race for time before the species are lost to deforestation. More often, the race is defined as being the first pharmaceutical company to patent a new drug utilizing a newly discovered rainforest phytochemical-and, of course, to garner the profits.

Indigenous People: A Valuable Resource

Laboratory synthesis of new medicines is increasingly costly and not as fruitful as companies would like. In the words of one major drug company executive, "Scientists may be able to make any molecule they can imagine on a computer, but Mother Nature . . . is an infinitely more ingenious and exciting chemist". Scientists have developed new technologies to assess the chemical makeup of plants, and they realize that using medicinal plants identified by Indians makes research more efficient and less expensive. With these new trends, drug development has actually returned to its roots: traditional medicine. It is now understood by bioprospectors that the tribal peoples of the rainforest represent the key to finding new and useful tropical forest plants. The degree to which these indigenous people understand and are able to use this diversity sustainably is astounding. A single Amazonian tribe of Indians may use more than 200 species of plants for medicinal purposes alone.

Of the 121 pharmaceutical drugs that are plant-derived today, 74 per cent were discovered through follow-up research to verify the authenticity of information concerning the medical uses of the plant by indigenous peoples. Nevertheless, to this day, very few rainforest tribes have been subjected to a complete ethnobotanical analysis. Researcher wrote, "Indigenous knowledge is essential for the use, identification and cataloguing of the [tropical] biota. As tribal groups disappear, their knowledge vanishes with them. The preservation of these groups is a significant economic opportunity for the [developing] nation, not a luxury."

Since Amazonian Indians are often the only ones who know both the properties of these plants and how they can best be used, their knowledge is now considered an essential component of all efforts to conserve and develop the rainforest. Since failure to document this lore would represent a tremendous economic and scientific loss to the industrialized world, the bioprospectors are now working side by side with the rainforest tribal shamans and herbal healers to learn the wealth of their plant knowledge. But bioprospecting has a dark side. Indian knowledge that has resisted the pressure of 'modernization' is being used by bioprospectors who, like oil companies and loggers destroying the forests, threaten to leave no benefits behind them.

But Few Benefits for the Indigenous People

It's a noble idea-the ethnobotanist working with the Indians seeking a cure for cancer or even AIDS, like Sean Connery in the movie Medicine Man. Yet behind this lurks a system that, at its worst, steals the Indian knowledge to benefit CEOs, stockholders, and academic careers and reputations. The real goal of these powerful bioprospectors is to target novel and active phytochemicals for medical applications, synthesize them in a laboratory, and have them patented for subsequent drug manufacture and resulting profits. In this process, many active and beneficial plants have been found in the shaman's medicine chest, only to be discarded when it was found that the active ingredients of the plant numbered too many to be cost effectively synthesized into a patentable drug. It doesn't matter how active or beneficial the plant is or how long the U.S. Food and Drug Administration (FDA) process might take to approve the new drug; if the bioprospector can't capitalize on it, the public will rarely hear about a plant's newly discovered benefits. The fact is there is a lot of money at stake. In an article published in Economic Botany, researchers, estimate the minimum number of pharmaceutical drugs potentially remaining to be extracted from the rainforests. It is staggering! They estimate that there are at least 328 new drugs that still await discovery in the rainforest, with a potential value of $3 billion to $4 billion to a private pharmaceutical company and as much as $147 billion to society as a whole.

While the indigenous Indian shamans go about their daily lives caring for the well-being of their tribe, the shaman's rainforest medicines are being tested, synthesized, patented, and submitted for FDA approval in U.S. laboratories thousands of miles away. Soon children with viral infections, adults with herpes, cancer patients, and many others may benefit from new medicines from the Amazon rainforest. But what will the indigenous tribes see of these wonderful new medicines? As corporations rush to patent indigenous medicinal knowledge, the originating indigenous communities receive few, if any, benefits.

The destruction of the rainforest has followed the pattern of seeing natural land and natural world peoples as resources to be used, and seeing wilderness as idle, empty, and unproductive. Destruction of our rainforests is not only causing the extinction of plant and animal species, it is also wiping out indigenous peoples who live in the rainforest. Obviously, rainforests are not idle land, nor are they uninhabited. Indigenous peoples have developed technologies and resource use systems that have allowed them to live on the land, farming, hunting, and gathering in a complex sustainable relationship with the forest. But when rainforests die, so do the indigenous peoples.

In 1500 there were an estimated 6 million to 9 million indigenous people inhabiting the rainforests in Brazil. When Western and European cultures were drawn to Brazil's Amazon in the hopes of finding riches beyond comprehension and artifacts from civilizations that have long since expired with the passage of time, they left behind decimated cultures in their ravenous wake. By 1900 there were only 1 million indigenous people left in Brazil's Amazon. Although the fabled Fountain of Youth was never discovered, many treasures in gold and gems were spirited away by the more successful invaders of the day, and the indigenous inhabitants of the rainforest bore the brunt of these marauding explorers and conquistadors.

Today there are fewer than 250,000 indigenous people of Brazil surviving this catastrophe, and still the destruction continues. These surviving indigenous people still demonstrate the remarkable diversity of the rainforest because they comprise 215 ethnic groups with 170 different languages. Nationwide, they live in 526 territories, which together compose an area of 190 million acres . . . twice the size of California. About 188 million acres of this land is inside the Brazilian Amazon, in the states of Acre, Amapa, Amazonas, Maranhao, Mato Grosso, Para, Rondonia, Roraima, and Tocantins. There may also be 50 or more indigenous groups still living in the depths of the rainforest that have never had contact with the outside world.

Throughout the rainforest, forest-dwelling peoples whose age-old traditions allow them to live in and off the forest without destroying it are losing out to cattle ranching, logging, hydroelectric projects, large-scale farms, mining, and colonization schemes. About half of the original Amazonian tribes have already been completely destroyed. The greatest threat to Brazil's remaining tribal people, most of whom live in the Amazon rainforest, is the invasion of their territory by ranchers, miners, and land speculators and the conflicts that follow. Thousands of peasants, rubber tappers, and indigenous tribes have been killed in Amazonia in the past decade in violent conflicts over forest resources and land.

As their homelands continue to be invaded and destroyed, rainforest people and their cultures are disappearing. When these indigenous peoples are lost forever, gone too will be their empirical knowledge representing centuries of accumulated knowledge of the medicinal value of plant and animal species in the rainforest. Very few tribes have been subjected to a complete ethnobotanical analysis of their plant knowledge, and most medicine men and shamans remaining in the rainforests today are seventy years old or more. When a medicine man dies without passing his arts on to the next generation, the tribe and the world lose thousands of years of irreplaceable knowledge about medicinal plants. Each time a rainforest medicine man dies, it is as if a library has burned down.

The problem and the solution of the destruction of the rainforest are both economic. Governments need money to service their debts, squatters and settlers need money to feed their families, and companies need to make profits.

The simple fact is that the rainforest is being destroyed for the income and profits it yields, however fleeting. Money still makes the world go around . . . even in South America and even in the rainforest. But this also means that if landowners, governments, and those living in the rainforest today were given a viable economic reason not to destroy the rainforest, it could and would be saved. And this viable economic alternative does exist, and it is working today.

Many organisations have demonstrated that if the medicinal plants, fruits, nuts, oils, and other resources like rubber, chocolate, and chicle (used to make chewing gums) are harvested sustainably, rainforest land has much more economic value today and more long-term income and profits for the future than if just timber is harvested or burned down for cattle or farming operations. In fact, the latest statistics prove that rainforest land converted to cattle operations yields the landowner $60 per acre; if timber is harvested, the land is worth $400 per acre. However, if medicinal plants, fruits, nuts, rubber, chocolate, and other renewable and sustainable resources are harvested, the land will yield the landowner $2,400 per acre. This value provides an income not only today, but year after year - for generations. These sustainable resources - not the trees - are the true wealth of the rainforest.

This is no longer a theory. It is a fact, and it is being implemented today. Just as important, to wild-harvest the wealth of sustainable rainforest resources effectively, local people and indigenous tribes must be employed.

Today entire communities and tribes earn five to ten times more money in wild-harvesting medicinal plants, fruits, nuts, and oils than they can earn by chopping down the forest for subsistence crops. This much-needed income source creates the awareness and economic incentive for this population in the rainforest to protect and preserve the forests for long-term profits for themselves and their children and is an important solution in saving the rainforest from destruction.

When the timber is harvested for short-term gain and profits, the medicinal plants, nuts, oils, and other important sustainable resources that thrive in this delicate ecosystem are destroyed. The real solution to saving the rainforest is to make its inhabitants see the forest and the trees by creating a consumer demand and consumer markets for these sustainable rainforest products . . . markets that are larger and louder than today's tropical timber market . . . markets that will put as much money in their pockets and government coffers as the timber companies do . . . markets that will give them the economic incentive to protect their sustainable resources for long-term profits, rather than short-term gain.

This is the only solution that makes a real impact, and it can make a real difference. Each and every person in the United States can take a part in this solution by helping to create this consumer market and demand for sustainable rainforest products. By purchasing renewable and sustainable rainforest products and resources and demanding sustainable harvesting of these resources using local communities and indigenous tribes of the rainforests, we all can be part of the solution, and the rainforests of the world and their people can be saved.

CHAPTER

The Importance of Forests

Forest Provides Multiple Benefits

Forest provides multiple benefits to environment, people, and animals. The list of benefits is as follows:

- Forest cool air temperature by release of water vapor into the air.
- At day time trees generate oxygen and store carbon dioxide, which helps to clean air.
- Forest attracts wild life and offer food and protection to them.
- Forests offer privacy, reduce light reflection, offer a sound barrier and help guide wind direction and speed.
- Trees offer artistic functions such as creating a background, framing a view, complementing architecture, and so on.
- Well managed forests supply higher quality water with less impurity than water from other resources.
- Some forests raise total water stream, but this is not true for all forests.
- Forests help in controlling the level floods.
- Forest provides different kind of wood which are used for different purposes like making of furniture, paper, and pencils and so on.

- Forest help in giving the direction of wind and its speed.
- Forest helps in keeping environment healthy and beautiful.
- Forests also minimize noise pollution.
- Forest helps the scientist to invent new medicine as forest has different kind or plants and herb.

Forest is a large area of land thickly covered with trees and bushes. Forests play very important role in building the economy of a country. They help to preserve agricultural land from the danger of erosion. Forests are the main source of timber for building and furniture as well as the firewood. Wood pulp is the primary source of raw material for paper industry. Forests also provide raw material for a number of other industries like sports goods and matches etc. Many kinds of pharmaceuticals, rayon and other useful materials like gums, resin, turpentine oil, are made from the raw material that can be found in forests. The trees also anchor the soil and prevent the winds from blowing the surface soil away. Rivers and streams receive water that flows down from very steep mountain rocks; forests on these slopes restrict the speed which would otherwise produce floods.

Forests Keep the Environment Pleasant

Forests keep the environment pleasant because they got moisture from earth through their roots and spread it in the air through their leaves. Decomposed leaves from humus which is the biggest source of soil fertility. Forests cause rainfall through the process of transpiration. Forests are the biggest source of oxygen which is essential for animals and plant life on the globe. Increasing green house effect is a growing menace for all sorts of life on the globe. Only forests can fight this danger in a very good manner.

Forests are a common heritage which have to be conserve due to its importance. The major importance of forests are:

1. Nature maintains a balance between carbondioxide and oxygen.
2. Forests trees helps in bringing sufficient rainfall on earth.

3. Forests are also helps in conservation of soil.
4. Forests provide habitat to wildlife and help in their preservation.
5. It provide food, medicinal herbs as well as other satisfactory requirement to fulfil our needs.

Forests are a Main Source of Oxygen

Forests are a main source of oxygen.they are the only source from which we can get oxygen to survive. Forests are also a source of wood and pulp from which we can make furniture and paper. They are also a precious resource so we should not do deforestation instead we should grow plants. It also serves as a shelter for different animals, birds and other micro-organisms.

Forest has been of great importance to mankind since prehistoric days. 60 per cent of the earth once covered with forest. With the development of civilization, large areas have been cleared to make way for farms, mines, towns and roads. Today about 30 per cent of earth is still forested.

The economic value of forests, supply many products like wood from trees as lumber, plywood and fuel wood or charcoal. Timber is used in furniture making, building houses, ships and railway sleepers. Pulp and paper are made from the cellulose of trees. Processed wood products include cellophane, plastics, synthetic fibres like rayon and nylon. Latex from trees such as the rubber tree goes to make tyres, tunes and a wide range of rubber goods.

Other uses; fruits, nuts and spices are gathered from the forest. Many medicinal plants such as camphor, cinchona, coca (from which the drug cocaine is extracted) also come from the forests. Cork from the thick bark of the cork oak is stripped for making bottling cork.

Conserve Soil

Forests help to conserve soil by preventing rapid runoff of water after heavy rain and minimizing flooding. Trees take in carbon dioxide and release oxygen into air, which is a great benefit to mankind.

Forests Influence Local and Global Climate

Forests influence local and global climate. The forest is also vital as a watershed. Because of the thick humus layer, loose soil, and soil-retaining powers of the trees' long roots, forests are vitally important for preserving adequate water supplies. The wild animals and other beings get enough protection from the solar heat, temperature and the leaf cover formed on the earth gives cooling effect to the earth. Since trees absorb heat, we shouldn't cut them down. Natural wildlife is important because it is part of the natural circle of life. If bears start to die off, (as it would be too hot without trees/forests) than the trout are going to become overpopulated and other scavengers that rely on bears will begin to starve. Without eagles and other birds of prey, rodents' population will increase which will cause more rodents in the cities and towns.

Forests offer privacy, reduce light reflection, offer a sound barrier and help guide wind direction and speed.

- Forest help in giving the direction of wind and its speed.
- Forest helps in keeping environment healthy and beautiful.
- Forests also minimize noise pollution.

Forests Supplies Food to Millions of People

Forests also provides raw materials to industries example: Timber, pharmaceutical, paper, etc.

Also promotes tourism, which is sourcwe of income for many local people.

Forests are natural habitat for wild life. Also provides timber for construction, for transport facilities. Plants are for pharmacy.

The most dangerous form of deforestation is the destruction of the rain forests, especially the tropical rain forests clustered around the equator. These are the most important sources of biological diversity on earth and the most vulnerable ecosystems now suffering the effects of our determined onslaught. Indeed, as many as half of all the living species on earth—some experts actually claim more than 90 per cent of all living species—find their homes in tropical rain forests, and the irretrievable loss of the living species dying along with them, represent the single most serious da age to nature now occurring. While some of the other injuries we are inflicting on the global ecological system may heal over the course of hundreds or thousands of years, the wholesale annihilation of so many living species in such a breathless moment of geological time represents a deadly wound to the integrity of the earth's painstakingly intricate web of life, a wound so nearly permanent that scientists estimate that recuperation would take 100 million years. Soil erosion is an inevitable result of deforestation. If you're asking the importance of a forest, a forest is important in many different ways. The leaves take in Carbon Dioxide and let out Oxygen, which we breathe in. They also provide a habitat for many types of different animals and nesting places for animals which reproduce. They provide food, medicinal herbs and many other requirements. Forests cool air temperature by release of water vapour into the air.

Forests deal with environmental issues:

1. They provide us oxygen and clean air by taking carbon dioxide and releasing oxygen.
2. They reduce pollution.
3. They help to increase moisture in air by transpiration and brings rainfall which helps to lower temperature.
4. The shade of trees prevents the excessive evaporation from soil not to become eroded or dry which further leads to the process of erosion.
5. It is a natural habitat for wildlife by providing food and shelter which help to maintain ecosystem.
6. The roots of the plants help to regulate or maintain the water level as rainwater can drain into ground through roots.
7. The roots of the trees helps or prevents soil to get eroded by either wind or rain.
8. It protects us from the flood and helps to lower the strength of wind during storms resulted in less damages.

CHAPTER 9

The Relationship Between the People and Forests

Forests Occupy Approximately One-third of Earth's Land Area

Today, forests occupy approximately one-third of Earth's land area, account for over two-thirds of the leaf area of land plants, and contain about 70 per cent of carbon present in living things. They have been held in reverence in folklore and worshipped in ancient religions. However, forests are becoming major casualties of civilization as human populations have increased over the past several thousand years, bringing deforestation, pollution, and industrial usage problems to this important biome.

About 420 million years ago, during the Silurian Period, ancient plants and arthropods began to occupy the land. Over the millions of years that followed, these land colonizers developed and adapted to their new habitat. The first forests were dominated by giant horsetails, club mosses, and ferns that stood up to 40 feet tall.

Life on Earth continued to evolve, and in the late Paleozoic, gymnosperms appeared. By the Triassic Period (245-208 mya), gymnosperms dominated the Earth's forests. In the Cretaceous Period (144-65 mya), the first flowering plants (angiosperms) appeared. They evolved together with insects, birds, and mammals and radiated rapidly, dominating the landscape by the end of the Period. The landscape changed again during the Pleistocene Ice Ages — the surface of the planet that had been dominated by tropical forests for millions of years changed, and temperate forests spread in the Northern Hemisphere.

Present-day forest biomes, biological communities that are dominated by trees and other woody vegetation can be classified according to numerous characteristics, with seasonality being the most widely used. Distinct forest types also occur within each of these broad groups.

There are three major types of forests, classed according to latitude:

- Tropical
- Temperate
- Boreal forests (taiga)
- Tropical forest

The Greatest Diversity of Species

Tropical forests are characterized by the greatest diversity of species. They occur near the equator, within the area bounded by latitudes 23.5° N and 23.5° S. One of the major characteristics of tropical forests is their distinct seasonality: winter is absent, and only two seasons are present (rainy and dry). The length of daylight is 12 hours and varies little.

- Temperature is on average 20-25° C and varies little throughout the year: the average temperatures of the three warmest and three coldest months do not differ by more than 5°.
- Precipitation is evenly distributed throughout the year, with annual rainfall exceeding 2000 mm.
- Soil is nutrient-poor and acidic. Decomposition is rapid and soils are subject to heavy leaching.
- Canopy in tropical forests is multilayered and continuous, allowing little light penetration.
- Flora is highly diverse: one square kilometre may contain as many as 100 different tree species. Trees are 25-35 m

tall, with buttressed trunks and shallow roots, mostly evergreen, with large dark green leaves. Plants such as orchids, bromeliads, vines (lianas), ferns, mosses, and palms are present in tropical forests.

- Fauna include numerous birds, bats, small mammals, and insects.

Further subdivisions of this group are determined by seasonal distribution of rainfall:

- *Evergreen rainforest*: no dry season.
- *Seasonal rainforest*: short dry period in a very wet tropical region (the forest exhibits definite seasonal changes as trees undergo developmental changes simultaneously, but the general character of vegetation remains the same as in evergreen rainforests).
- *Semievergreen forest*: longer dry season (the upper tree story consists of deciduous trees, while the lower story is still evergreen).
- *Moist/dry deciduous forest (monsoon)*: the length of the dry season increases further as rainfall decreases (all trees are deciduous).

More than one half of tropical forests have already been destroyed.

Temperate Forest

Temperate forests occur in eastern North America, northeastern Asia, and western and central Europe. Well-defined seasons with a distinct winter characterize this forest biome. Moderate climate and a growing season of 140-200 days during 4-6 frost-free months distinguish temperate forests.

- Temperature varies from –30° C to 30° C.
- Precipitation (75-150 cm) is distributed evenly throughout the year.
- Soil is fertile, enriched with decaying litter.
- Canopy is moderately dense and allows light to penetrate, resulting in well-developed and richly diversified understory vegetation and stratification of animals.

- Flora is characterized by 3-4 tree species per square kilometre. Trees are distinguished by broad leaves that are lost annually and include such species as oak, hickory, beech, hemlock, maple, basswood, cottonwood, elm, willow, and spring-flowering herbs.
- Fauna is represented by squirrels, rabbits, skunks, birds, deer, mountain lion, bobcat, timber wolf, fox, and black bear.

Further subdivisions of this group are determined by seasonal distribution of rainfall:

- *Moist conifer and evergreen broad-leaved forests*: wet winters and dry summers (rainfall is concentrated in the winter months and winters are relatively mild).
- *Dry conifer forests*: dominate higher elevation zones; low precipitation.
- *Mediterranean forests*: precipitation is concentrated in winter, less than 1000 mm per year.
- *Temperate coniferous*: mild winters, high annual precipitation (greater than 2000 mm).
- *Temperate broad-leaved rainforests*: mild, frost-free winters, high precipitation (more than 1500 mm) evenly distributed throughout the year. Only scattered remnants of original temperate forests remain.

Indigenous forest people use their land in many different ways – for fishing, hunting, shifting agriculture, the gathering of wild forest products and other activities. For them, the forest is the very basis of survival and its resources have to be harvested in a sustainable manner. But when traditional life styles change and, for example, industrial logging or mining takes place, over use of resources can lead to conflict.

Although indigenous people around the world often have very different sets of beliefs and traditions, a special bond with the land is a common factor. For example, the semi-nomadic Matses people of the Peruvian Amazon call the rainforest Titá, or mother referring to Titá as if to a person, who can be happy as well as sad, angry as well as indifferent.

Titá provides the Matses with everything they need – as long as they follow her rules, including never taking more from the forest than is needed and treating all things belonging to it with respect. Traditionally, the Matses perform hunting ceremonies to ask the animal spirits for permission to kill animals for food.

As with the Matses, indigenous peoples' ideas of territory are not only concerned with controlling a geographical area or using forest resources: territory also embodies fundamental aspects of culture and geography.

Indigenous forest people see themselves as inseparably linked to the forest and everything in it – trees, plants, rivers, animals and mountains. It is impossible, according to community beliefs, to separate any single object or living thing in the forest – such as a particular plant, animal or mineral – from its symbolic position in the cosmoogy of the people. These ideas are expressed through mythology, religious practices, and systems of social regulation, including management of the environment and systems of production and exchange Because of their special relationship with the land, many indigenous people cannot comprehend the idea that forests and land can be bought and sold.

However this does not mean they do not have a clear notion of their rights. The use of certain areas or resources may be granted based on a number of criteria, such as belonging to a particular group, tribe or clan. Land use can also be based on reciprocal agreements with neighbouring groups or individuals.

In many countries, the State is the official owner of most forest areas, even though some of the land may have been inhabited for generations by large numbers of people. In some cases the rights of those people are recognized.

In the Philippines for example, land issues in those areas are governed by the Indigenous Peoples' Rights Act.

Unfortunately such regulations are often contravened by powerful local interests. Also, traditional tenure systems are not always recognized by governments, leaving indigenous forest people without formal rights to their territories.

This violates the United Nations Declaration on Indigenous Peoples' Rights (UNDIPR) as well as ILO Convention 169 – both of which place a clear obligation on States to legally recognize, demarcate and effectively protect indigenous peoples' territories and natural resources.

Forest Biomes Represent the Largest and Most Ecologically Complex Systems

Forest Biomes represent the largest and most ecologically complex systems. They contain a wide assortment of trees, plants, mammals, reptiles, amphibians, invertebrates, insects and micro-organisms which vary depending on the zone's climates. Sadly, boreal and rainforest biomes are being cut down at an alarming rate, with hundreds of species of plants and animals disappearing from the planet on a daily basis. Forests represent a third of the earth's land, and are found in the four corners of the globe. The major attribute of the forest biome is its trees. While they are different from animals in many ways, they share one common characteristic: they breathe. While humans and animals breathe in oxygen and exhale carbon dioxide, trees take in carbon dioxide and produce oxygen. Deforestation represents a great threat to the future of the earth's atmosphere, and the only way this can be avoided is by careful management of this resource. Once a tree is cut down, another should take its place, but there is still too large a number of trees being cut down as opposed to the number of trees being planted.

The largest of the land biomes is the boreal, or Taiga biome. Taiga biomes can be found in areas with shorter, warm summers and long winters; there are Taiga Biomes in Europe, Asia, Siberia, and North-America. Because of the cold climates, plant life in the boreal forest is sturdy, consisting mainly of evergreens and other resilient vegetation. Because the forests' canopy is dense, forest floor vegetation is thin. Animal life in the boreal forest consists mainly of birds and mammals, such as deer, wolves, and various rodents, and very few reptiles. Most of the boreal forests' creatures are well adapted to the cold climate, and hibernate during the long winters.

Temperate deciduous forest are a close relative of the Taiga biome, and can be found in areas with a milder, shorter winter season. In addition to evergreens, trees in the temperate forest include maple, elm, oak, cedar and other trees which shed their leaves in the fall. The temperate forest's soil in richer than that of the boreal forests' and features a larger assortment of forest floor plan life; this is also due to the fact that the forests' canopy is thinner, allowing more light and heat to penetrate, permitting photosynthesis in the forest floor plants, and the survival of smaller, and cold blooded animals such as garter snakes, turtles, and a few amphibians. Again, several of the temperate forests' species hibernate, and/or burrow in the ground to pass the winter months.

Other forests which fall between the boreal and temperate classification include moist evergreen forests, moist evergreen and broad-leaf forests, dry evergreen forests, mediterranean forests, temperate evergreen forests, and temperate broad-leaf forests.

Forests can be found in all regions capable of sustaining tree growth, at altitudes up to the tree line, except where natural fire frequency or other disturbance is too high, or where the environment has been altered by human activity.

The latitudes 10° north and south of the Equator are mostly covered in tropical rainforest, and the latitudes between 53°N and 67°N have boreal forest. As a general rule, forests dominated by angiosperms (*broadleaf forests*) are more species-rich than those dominated by gymnosperms (*conifer*, *montane*, or *needleleaf forests*), although exceptions exist.

One strategy which is increasingly being used by forest people in order to defend their rights is to provide proof of their residence in, and use of, forest areas. In the Democratic Republic of the Congo, indigenous groups and other forest-dependent communities are participating in the mapping of their traditional territories. Such maps are likely to be a vital tool in the future as indigenous people around the world struggle to gain formal recognition of their rights. More than 1.6 billion people around the world depend to varying degrees on forests for their livelihoods – not just for food but also for fuel, for livestock grazing areas and for medicine. At least 350 million people live inside or close to dense forests, largely dependent on these areas for subsistence and income, while about 60 million indigenous people are almost wholly dependent on forests.

CHAPTER

The Wildlife of India

Different Types of Organism

The wildlife of India is a mix of species of number of different types of organism. The region's rich and diverse wildlife is preserved in 89 national parks, 13 Bio reserves and 400+ wildlife sanctuaries across the country. Since India is home to a number of rare and threatened animal species, wildlife management in the country is essential to preserve these species. According to one study, India along with 17 mega diverse countries is home to about 60-70 per cent of the world's biodiversity.

India, lying within the Indomalaya ecozone, is home to about 7.6 per cent of all mammalian, 12.6 per cent of avian, 6.2 per cent of reptilian, and 6.0 per cent of flowering plant species. Many ecoregions, such as the *shola* forests, also exhibit extremely high rates of endemism; overall, 33 per cent of Indian plant species are endemic. India's forest cover ranges from the tropical rainforest of the Andaman Islands, Western Ghats, and Northeast India to the coniferous forest of the Himalaya. Between these extremes lie the sal-dominated moist deciduous forest of eastern India; teak-dominated dry deciduous forest of central and southern India; and the babul-dominated thorn forest of the central Deccan and western Gangetic plain. Important Indian trees include the medicinal neem, widely used in rural Indian herbal remedies. The pipal fig tree, shown on the seals of Mohenjo-daro, shaded the Gautama Buddha as he sought enlightenment.

Many Indian species are descendants of taxa originating in Gondwana, to which India originally belonged. Peninsular India's subsequent movement towards, and collision with, the Laurasian landmass set off a mass exchange of species. However, volcanism and climatic change 20 million years ago caused the extinction of many endemic Indian forms. Soon thereafter, mammals entered India from Asia through two zoogeographical passes on either side of the emerging Himalaya. As a result, among Indian species, only 12.6 per cent of mammals and 4.5 per cent of birds are endemic, contrasting with 45.8 per cent of reptiles and 55.8 per cent of amphibians. Notable endemics are the Nilgiri leaf monkey and the brown and carmine Beddome's toad of the Western Ghats. India contains 172, or 2.9 per cent, of IUCN-designated threatened species. These include the Asiatic lion, the Bengal tiger, and the Indian white-rumped vulture, which suffered a near-extinction from ingesting the carrion of diclofenac-treated cattle.

In recent decades, human encroachment has posed a threat to India's wildlife; in response, the system of national parks and protected areas, first established in 1935, was substantially expanded. In 1972, India enacted the Wildlife Protection Act and Project Tiger to safeguard crucial habitat; further federal protections were promulgated in the 1980s. Along with over 500 wildlife sanctuaries, India now hosts 15 biosphere reserves, four of which are part of the World Network of Biosphere Reserves; 25 wetlands are registered under the Ramsar Convention.

The varied and rich wildlife of India has had a profound impact on the region's popular culture. The common name for wilderness in India is Jungle, which was adopted into the English language. The word has been also made famous in *'The Jungle Book'* by researcher. India's wildlife has been the subject of numerous other tales and fables such as the *Panchatantra* and the *Jataka tales*.

Fauna of India

India is home to several well known large mammals including the Asian Elephant, Bengal Tiger, Asiatic Lion, Leopard, Sloth Bear and Indian Rhinoceros, often engrained culturally and religiously often being associated with deities. Other well known large Indian mammals include ungulates such as the rare Wild Asian Water buffalo, common Domestic Asian Water buffalo, Nilgai, Gaur and several species of deer and antelope. Some members of the dog family such as the Indian Wolf, Bengal Fox, Golden Jackal and the (ow the world's rarest monkey, the golden langur typifies the precarious survival of much of India's megafauna.)

The need for conservation of wildlife in India is often questioned because of the apparently incorrect priority in the face of direct poverty of the people. However Article 48 of the Constitution of India specifies that, "The state shall endeavour to protect and improve the environment and to safeguard the forests and wildlife of the country" and Article 51-A states that "it shall be the duty of every citizen of India to protect and improve the natural environment including forests, lakes, rivers, and wildlife and to have compassion for living creatures".

Large and charismatic mammals are important for wildlife tourism in India and several national parks and wildlife sanctuaries cater to these needs. Project Tiger started in 1972 is a major effort to conserve the tiger and its habitats. At the turn of the 20th century, one estimate of the tiger population in India placed the figure at 40,000, yet an Indian tiger census conducted in 2008 revealed the existence of only 1411 tigers. The passing of the Forest Rights Act by the Indian government in 2008 has been the final nail in the coffin and has pushed the Indian tiger on the verge of extinction.Various pressures in the later part of the 20th century led to the progressive decline of wilderness resulting in the disturbance of viable tiger habitats. At the International Union for the Conservation of Nature and Natural Resources (IUCN) General Assembly meeting in Delhi in 1969, serious concern was voiced about the threat to several species of wildlife and the shrinkage of wilderness in the India. In 1970, a national ban on tiger hunting was imposed and in 1972 the Wildlife Protection Act came into force. The framework was then set up to formulate a project for tiger conservation with an ecological approach.

Launched on April 1, 1973, Project Tiger has become one of the most successful conservation ventures in modern history. The project aims at tiger conservation in specially constituted 'tiger reserves' which are representative of various bio-geographical regions falling within India. It strives to maintain a viable tiger population in their natural environment. Today, there are 39 Project Tiger wildlife reserves in India covering an area more than of 37,761 km^2.

Recent Extinctions

The exploitation of land and forest resources by humans along with hunting and trapping for food and sport has led to the extinction of many species in India in recent times. These species include mammals such as the Indian/Asiatic Cheetah, Wild Zebu, Javan Rhinoceros and Sumatran Rhinoceros. While some of these large mammal species are confirmed extinct, there have been many smaller animal and plant species whose status is harder to determine. Many species have not been seen since their description. The Bengal Tigers in India, although they are threatened to extinction.

Hubbardia heptaneuron, a species of grass that grew in the spray zone of the Jog Falls prior to the construction of the Linganamakki reservoir, was thought to be extinct but a few were rediscovered near Kolhapur.

Some species of birds have gone extinct in recent times, including the Pink-headed Duck (*Rhodonessa caryophyllacea*) and the Himalayan Quail (*Ophrysia superciliosa*). A species of warbler, *Acrocephalus orinus*, known earlier from a single specimen collected by Allan Octavian Hume from near Rampur in Himachal Pradesh was rediscovered after 139 years in Thailand.

Fungi of India

The diversity of fungi and their natural beauty occupy a prime place in the biological world and India has been a cradle for such organisms. Only a fraction of the total fungal wealth of India has been subjected to scientific scrutiny and mycologists have to unravel this unexplored and hidden wealth. One-third of fungal diversity of the globe exists in India. The country has an array of 10 diverse biomes including Trans-Himalayan zone, Himalaya, Desert, Semi-Arid zone, Western Ghats, Deccan Peninsula, Gangetic Plain, North-Eastern India, Coasts and Islands where varied dominating regimes manifest. This enables the survival of manifold fungal flora in these regions which include hot spot areas like the Himalayan ranges, Western Ghats, hill stations, mangroves, sea coasts, fresh water bodies etc. Many fungi have been recorded from these regions and from the country in general comprising thermophiles, psychrophiles, mesophiles, aquatic forms, marine forms, plant and animal pathogens, edible fungi and beneficial fungi and so on. The number of fungi recorded in India exceeds 27,000 species, the largest biotic community after insects. The true fungi belong to the Kingdom Fungi which has four phyla, 103 orders, 484 families and 4979 genera. About 205 new genera have been described from India, of which 32 per cent were discovered by researcher. These features indicate a ten-fold increase in the last 70 years.

Flora of India

There are about 17500 taxa of flowering plants from India. The Indian Forest Act, 1927 helped to improve protection of the natural habitat.

Biosphere Reserves

The Indian government has established seventeen Biosphere Reserves of India which protect larger areas of natural habitat and often include one or more National Parks and/or preserves, along buffer zones that are open to some economic uses. Protection is granted not only to the flora and fauna of the protected region, but also to the human communities who inhabit these regions, and their ways of life. The Bio-reserves in India are:

- Achanakmar-Amarkantak
- Agasthyamalai
- Dibru Saikhowa
- Dihang Dibang
- Great Nicobar
- Gulf of Mannar
- Kachchh
- Kangchenjunga
- Manas
- Nanda Devi
- The Nilgiris
- Nokrek
- Pachmarhi
- Simlipal
- Sundarbans
- Cold desert
- Seshachalam hills

Seven of the fifteen biosphere reserves are a part of the World Network of Biosphere Reserves, based on the UNESCO Man and the Biosphere Programme (MAB) list.

- Gulf of Mannar biosphere reserve
- Nanda Devi biosphere reserve
- Nilgiri biosphere reserve
- Nokrek national park
- Pachmarhi biosphere reserve
- Simlipal national park
- Sundarbans biosphere reserve

CHAPTER

Loss of Forests

Deforestation began thousands of years ago for building ships and houses. However, over the last 20 years, more than 300 million hectares of tropical forests (an area larger than the size of India) have been cleared for plantations, agriculture, pasture, mining, or urban development. Today forests cover only half of the area they did when agriculture began 11,000 years ago. This earlier loss of 50 per cent of the Earth's forests is sufficient, in itself, to severely disrupt the global carbon cycle.

God has cared for these trees, saved them from drought, disease, avalanches, and a thousand tempests and floods. But he cannot save them from fools.

The amount of global forest cover is a key indicator of the health of the planet. An intact forest cycles nutrients, regulates climate, stabilizes soil, treats waste, provides habitat, and offers opportunities for recreation. Forests also help regulate local and regional rainfall, are sources of food, medicine, clean drinking water and they provide immense recreational, aesthetic, and spiritual benefits.

World Resources Institute estimates that, at current deforestation rates, about 40 per cent of today's intact forests will be gone within 10-20 years. The loss of these trees results in fewer trees to absorb carbon dioxide, and the cut trees release the carbon that had been stored in them.

Rainforests Cover Two Per cent of the Earth's Surface

Rainforests cover two per cent of the earth's surface, or 6 per cent of its land mass, yet they house over half the plant and animal species on Earth. They originally covered at least twice that area.

Consequences of Deforestation

Removing forests (and their natural functions) causes many serious problems. Removing forests (and their natural functions) causes many serious problems.

- *Loss of trees makes global warming worse.* Through photosynthesis, trees remove carbon dioxide from the air, produce oxygen, and store carbon as wood. One ton of carbon in wood or forest biomass represents 3.67 tons of atmospheric carbon dioxide recycled. We are creating warming, not only by putting more CO_2 into the air, but also by getting rid of trees that absorb and remove carbon from the air.
- *Impact on Ecosystems.* Forests preserve water, soils, plants and wildlife. Their destruction aggravates droughts, soil erosion, and pollution of watercourses, and causes extensive flooding, and increased pest populations due to the ecological imbalance.
- *Loss of Species.* Tropical forests contain at least half the Earth's species, so their loss causes a dramatic loss of biodiversity. *Clearing and destructive logging of forests is the single greatest cause of species extinction worldwide.*
- *Harm to Water.* Forests are natural dams that catch rainwater in their canopies and in leaves and litter on the forest floor, retaining and purifying rainwater. Forest logging allows rapid run-off and destroys the ability of the soil to absorb water.

It's one thing not to see the forest for the trees, but then to go on to deny the reality of the forest is a more serious matter.

Causes and Motives for Deforestation

Among the direct causes of deforestation, some of the main ones are: the substitution of forests by other activities (agriculture, cattle-raising, tree plantations, shrimp farming, etc.), logging, mining, oil exploitation, and construction of large hydroelectric dams (which result in the flooding of extensive areas of forest).

Forests are Cleared for Agriculture

The deforestation rate in Amazon rainforest, the world's largest jungle, jumped 40 per cent in the 12 months to the middle of 2002. The Amazon is an area of continuous tropical forest just under half the size of the continental United States, and has been described as the 'lungs of the world' because of its vast capacity to produce oxygen. It is also home to up to 30 per cent of the planet's animal and plant species.

The Primary Driving Force Behind the Destruction of the Rainforests is Livestock Grazing

Beef exporting from Brazil has increased more than fivefold in the last six years. *Worldwatch* magazine, in the article, 'Eating Beef' states that "From now on, the question of whether we get our protein from animals or plants has direct implications for how much more of the world's remaining forest we have to raze."

Forests are Destroyed by Inequitable Land Policies

International finance institutions require countries to increase exports in order to keep up with their loan payments, and clear-cutting the forests for crops is often their only option. The agricultural land of peasants is taken over to increase exports, forcing them to migrate into the forests where they cut and burn the forest in order to survive. In many cases, governments promote migration to expand the agricultural frontier and allow for more farm exports.

Global Warming Threatens Forests Worldwide

Deforestation contributes to global warming, but, in turn, global warming will increase the loss of forests. Many of the world's forests are in poor condition, fragmented, and degradated, and so they are less able to adapt or adjust to climate change. As the global climate warms up, patterns of rainfall will change; and 'normal' temperature patterns will be disrupted. The expected rate of global warming and sea-level rise will be too fast to allow most forests to be able to adapt quickly enough to survive.

The organisation, American Forests, reports that the U.S. could offset 20 to 40 per cent of its carbon dioxide emissions by increasing carbon storage by 300-600 million tons per year. This would require a comprehensive plan to plant trees, improved forest management practices, and alternatives to wood and biomass fuels.

Each Year, Forest Fires, Burn Between Six and Fourteen Million Hectares of Forest

A major cause of the loss and degradation of forested land comes from fire. The area lost to fire is roughly equal to that caused by destructive logging and conversion to agriculture combined. Severe forest fires, such as those in Indonesia in 1997/1998 and in Australia in 2001/2002, bring enormous and in some cases life-threatening levels of pollutants. Governments rarely address the underlying causes of forest fires. Instead of prevention efforts, they just work to put the fires out. Working on prevention will become essential because global warming will increase the number of forest fires.

Forests are Harmed by the Trade in Illegally Extracted Timber

Legal supplies of wood fibre fall short of demand by up to 40 million cubic metres per year. Illegal logging fills the gap—accounting for almost 70 per cent of wood supply, meaning that illegal logging *exceeds* the volume of legal logging. All told, illegal logging alone has destroyed 10 million hectares of Indonesia's rich forests, an area the size of Virginia.

It is important to use only wood certified by the Forest Stewardship Council (FSC)—the only label recognized as providing 'ecologically-sound' timber. Worldwide, FSC-accrediting bodies have certified about 24 million hectares of forests in 45 countries. When consumers demand certified wood, non-certified sellers will have difficulty competing, and illegal logging becomes more difficult. This certification stamp means the wood is from well-managed and environmentally sensitive logging operations. It also assures that the wood is not the result of monoculture plantations, clear-cutting, violations of indigenous land claims, or other environmental hazards. Due to these other considerations, relying on wood labeled 'second-growth' is not enough. The FSC label is the only guarantee that the wood purchased is environmentally sound. Currently only a small portion of the U.S. lumber market, FSC wood is growing in popularity in other areas, especially in Europe.

Building Large Hydroelectric Dams Destroys Forests

Forests are lost when farmers, displaced by dams being built, are forced to move and clear forests in other areas in order to grow their crops. Dams also require road building, allowing access to previously remote areas by loggers and 'developers', causing even more deforestation.

Forests are Cleared for Fuel or Export

Crucial to slowing the loss of the world's natural forests is finding alternative sources of energy for low-income countries so that wood is not burned for energy.

Of all the wonders of nature, a tree in summer is perhaps the most remarkable; with the possible exception of a moose singing 'Embraceable You' in spats.

Policies Needed to Halt Deforestation

Despite the creation of new organisations to promote sustainable forestry, and continuing efforts of major international conservation organisations, the rate of forest loss accelerated through the 1990s.

Deforestation is driven by a wide range of social and economic forces, but underlying them all is the relentless march of *human population growth* and the exponentially rising demand for land and forest products such growth generates. These demands are not going to slacken in the decades ahead; indeed, they will only expand. Slowing down tropical deforestation, much less halting it will therefore entail bucking powerful and inexorably growing forces. It is in this stark light that the prospects for conserving tropical forests must be considered.

Extinction of Plant and Animal Species

Massive extinctions have occurred *five times* during the earth's history, the last one was the extinction of the dinosaurs, 65 million years ago. Scientists are calling what is occurring now, the *sixth mass extinction*. The loss of species is about losing *the very web of life* on Earth. People trying to save critical habitat have been dismissed or ridiculed as sentimental 'tree-huggers' who want to save the 'spotted owls', even if it costs jobs. Most Americans have little idea of the magnitude of the problem.

Although they are uncertain of the numbers, most scientists believe the *rate of loss* is greater now than at any time in the history of the Earth. Within the next 30 years as many as *half of the species on the earth* could die in one of the fastest mass extinctions in the planet's 4.5 billion years history. Dr Leakey, author of "The Sixth Extinction," believes that 50 per cent of the earth's species will vanish within 100 years and that such a dramatic and overwhelming mass extinction threatens the entire, complex fabric of life, including *Homo sapiens*, (the species responsible for the crisis.)

The problem is not just the loss of species. There is also the loss of the genetic diversity *within* species, as well as the loss of diversity of different types of *ecosystems*,which can contribute to or hasten whole species extinction. Preserving the wider gene pool diversity in subdivisions of species, such as subspecies and populations, offers the raw material for the evolution of new species in the future.

> "Every day, an estimated 100 plant and animal species are lost to deforestation" . . . "A conservative estimate of the current extinction rate indicates that about 27,000 species a year are being lost."
>
> —*National Wildlife Federation*

Causes of the Extinction of Species

Scientists have identified the key causes of the crisis. In particular, the loss of species is caused by as the growing size of human populations, and the rate at which humans consume resources and cause changing climate.

Global Warming and the Loss of Species

At the end of the Permian period, 251 million years ago, g lobal warming caused the worst mass extinction in the history of the planet. That time a six-degree C. increase in the global temperature was enough to kill up to 95 per cent of the species that were alive on Earth. This extinction is called the 'Great Dying'. Gigantic volcanic eruptions caused this warming by triggering a 'runaway greenhouse effect' that nearly put an end to life on Earth. Conditions in what geologists have termed a 'post-apocalyptic greenhouse' were so severe that only one large land animal was left alive, and fewer than one in 10 species survived.

It took *100 million years* for species diversity to return to former levels. In this case, the carbon dioxide buildup which created this greenhouse effect came from massive volcanic eruptions. Today the build up of carbon dioxide is coming from our life style and industrial activity.

An increase of 6°C is the upper end of what the IPCC is forecasting for this century, the range that will occur if we do not make severe changes soon. If 95 per cent of the species on Earth die out—one of them will be *Homo sapiens.*

Global Warming is Already Affecting Species

Migration is accelerating, the timing of the seasons is changing, and animals are migrating, hatching eggs, and bearing young on average five days earlier than they did at the start of the 20th century. In addition, some butterflies have shifted northward in Europe by thirty to sixty miles or more, species' ranges are shifting toward the poles at some four miles a decade, amphibians were spawning earlier, and plants are flowering earlier. In a major report in *Nature*, the author said: There is a consistent signal. Animals and plants are being strongly affected by the warming of the globe. It was really quite a shock, given such a small temperature change . . . If we're already seeing such dramatic changes among species, it's really pretty frightening to think what we might see in the next 100 years.

For if one link in nature's chain might be lost, another might be lost, until the whole of things will vanish by piecemeal.

Habitat Loss as a Cause of the Loss of Species

Other than global warming, the greatest threat to biodiversity is habitat loss and fragmentation by deforestation and urbanization.

Urbanization has dramatically increased the rate of habitat loss and change. Sprawling development is consuming land at a rate of five or more times the rate of population growth, destroying wildlife habitat and degrading water quality. Dredging, draining, bulldozing, and paving the land for housing developments, malls, business parks, and new roads, all destroy habitat. For example, in Maryland, 10 years ago every new person added to the state accounted for the loss of 1/3 acre of land; now, every new person causes the loss of 2/3 acre.

Biological resources are degraded and lost through 'development' activities like large-scale clearing and burning of forests, over-harvesting of plants and animals, use of pesticides, draining and filling of wetlands, destructive fishing practices, air pollution, and the conversion of wildlands to agricultural and urban uses.

Humans Create all of these Causes

Humans have altered nearly *half* of Earth's land mass over the past 150 years and the amount could rise to 70 per cent within 30 years, according to the United Nation. These alterations include farming, logging and urban development.

Deforestation

Deforestation is also one of the leading causes of habitat loss. For centuries, humans have altered landscapes, through deforestation, fire and over-use. Already, around half of the world's original forests have disappeared, and they are still being removed at a rate 10 times higher than any possible level of re-growth. As tropical forests contain at least half the Earth's species, the clearance of some 17 million hectares each year is causing a dramatic loss of biodiversity. Habitat loss is identified as a main threat to 85 per cent of all species described in the IUCN's *Red Lists* (those species officially classified as 'threatened' and 'endangered'. ICUN is the World Conservation Union").

Invasive Alien Species Cause the Loss of Species

An 'alien' or 'exotic' species is one that occurs in an area outside its historically known natural range, as a result of either intentional or accidental dispersal by human activities. For millennia, oceans, mountains, rivers and deserts served as natural barriers to the movement of certain plants and animals, providing the isolation essential for unique species and ecosystems to evolve. In just a few hundred years, however, international trade and the expansion of global travel, accompanied by intentional introductions, have ended millions of years of biological isolation. When alien animal and plant species spread to non-native habitats, they alter habitats, and crowd out native species through predation, competition, disease and hybridisation. Hundreds, possibly thousands of extinctions have been caused by alien invasive species.

Pollution Leads to a Loss of Species

Pollution is found everywhere in the world—chemicals have been found in animals even in the Arctic and Antarctic. Chemicals can cause mutations and fertility problems, already seen in the reproductive organs of fish, alligators, and polar bears. The city and industry sewage treatment plants that lack advanced technology, dump nutrients and pathogens in the water. When the treatment plants discharging into Tampa Bay were upgraded, the sea grasses, 85 per cent of which had been destroyed, began to grow back, and along with them the fish and other creatures that depend on them.

A recent EPA report noted that nearly 40 per cent of the nation's rivers, lakes, and estuaries are too polluted for safe fishing and swimming. Fifty per cent of freshwater species populations, from fish and frogs to river dolphins, are declining from pollution by pesticides, fertilizers and other agricultural chemicals. Everything that happens on land affects the waterways; storm water picks up contaminants from roads, vehicles, lawns, and construction sites and then dumps it in the nearest stream.

In pushing other species to extinction, humanity is busy sawing off the limb on which it is perched".

Bycatch Causes the Loss of Species

Bycatch is unwanted species, juveniles, and other marine wildlife, that fishers catch unintentionally. Commercial fishing is grossly wasteful: in the process of harvesting 85 million tons of fish each year, fishers routinely discard at least 20 million tons of 'bycatch', unwanted fish and marine specs that are usually killed.

According to a new study submitted to the International Whaling Commission (IWC), nearly 1,000 whales, dolphins, and porpoises drown *every day* when they become entangled in fishing gear,. Scientists believe that death in fishing gear is the leading threat to the survival of the world's 80-plus species of whales, dolphins and porpoises. Bycatch is also the greatest threat to seabirds and sea turtles.

Illegal Wildlife Trade Causes the Loss of Species

Trade in some animal and plant species is high, and is capable of heavily depleting their populations and even bringing some species close to extinction. Live animals are taken for the pet trade, or their parts exported for medicines or food. Thousands of species including African and Asian elephants, Tibetan antelopes, rhinos, birds of paradise, parrots, and orchids are part of the illegal international wildlife trade. This trade is worth billions of dollars annually and has caused massive declines in the numbers of many species of animals and plants.

The scale of over-exploitation for trade is a major threat to the survival of species. In 1973, to try to stop this trade, an international treaty (CITES, Convention on International Trade in Endangered Species of Wild Fauna and Flora) was created that subjected international trade in specimens of selected species to certain controls.

CHAPTER

Endangered Animals of the World

Endangered means to be under threat or near extinction. When a species/animal is endangered it means that they are disappearing fast or have a very small population - not large enough to survive. Extinction means the end of existence for a species.

Greater Horseshoe Bat – (*Rhinolophus ferrumequinum*)

- *IUCN Status:* least concern
- *Population trend:* decreasing

There are eighteen species of bat in Britain and all of them are endangered. The greater horseshoe bat is one of the rarest. One reason for their decline is the destruction of suitable roosting sites, such as old buildings and hollow trees. Changing land use from woodland and small fields to large scale agriculture has also had an effect. They have also suffered from the use of insecticides (poisonous chemicals sprayed on to crops to kill harmful insects) which have deprived the bats of their insect food. Due to conservation efforts its population in the UK has stabilized at about 5000.

Siberian (Amur) Tiger – (*Panthera tigris* ssp. altaica)

- *IUCN status:* endangered
- *Population trend:* stable

Cold, snowy Siberia, Russia, is home to the largest of all the tigers, the Siberian tiger.

It is highly endangered although its numbers have increased from an all time low of 20 in the 1930s. There are now an estimated 360 Amur tigers in the wild, according to the IUCN. Hunting and loss of habitat have reduced their numbers and there is little genetic diversity in the remaining population, increasing their vulnerability There is also a tiny population remaining in China of around 20 individuals.

Loggerhead Turtle (*Caretta caretta*)

- *IUCN Status:* endangered

This threatened reptile lives in the Mediterranean Sea, as well as the Black Sea and Atlantic Ocean. In the past its main dangers were hunting for its shell and meat. Now it has to put up with tourists disturbing the sandy beaches where it lays its eggs. In Turkey, hotels have been built right on its breeding sites. Out at sea, the turtles sometimes become entangled in fishing nets and drown. A possible new threat to them may be the increase in sand temperatures which determines the sex of the turtle. Warmer temperatures could result in an excess of females!

Northern Bald Ibis (*Geronticus eremita*)

- *IUCN Status:* critically endangered.
- *Population trend:* decreasing

Morocco is home to 95 per cent of the truly wild colonies of the ibis where populations are increasing and now number over 500 birds. Syria also has a small and declining population with only 5 mature birds. Parts of North Africa and the Middle East are visited by these migrating birds. Turkey also have a healthy semi-wild population of reintroduced birds, numbering 91 in 2006 (IUCN). However, the use of pesticides on the marshes and grasslands where it lives is reducing the numbers.

Part of the ibis' decline is due to natural causes. It nests high above the ground and its eggs are so round that some of them roll out of the nest and break. However disturbance of nesting sites and feeding grounds is a more significant factor.

The Ancient Egyptians used to depict this bird in their heiroglyphic writing, but it no longer lives in Egypt.

White Tailed Eagle (*Haliaeetus albicilla*)

- *IUCN Status:* least concern
- *Population trend:* increasing

5,000-6,000 breeding pairs in Europe. An estimated global population of 20,300-39,600. (IUCN).

Before man began polluting wetland habitats with pesticides, this spectacular bird of prey was much more numerous than it is today. In the Middle East, its population is now very small. The bird travels long distances in search of fish, and eating a number of poisoned fish causes the bird to lay infertile or thin-shelled eggs which are easily broken. Modern forestry methods result in a loss of suitable nesting places. They became extinct in Britain in the early 1900s due to persecution but are now breeding in Scotland since they were reintroduced in 1975.

Lion-Tailed Macaque (*Macaca silenus*)

- *IUCN Status:* endangered
- *Population trend:* decreasing
- *Population:* less than 4,000

This small small monkey is only found in south-west India's tropical rainforests. Many of these forests have been cleared and replaced with tea and coffee plantations. Unlike some other animals, the lion-tailed macaque has not been able to adapt to these new habitats. Poachers have also captured baby macaques, often killing their parents in the process, for illegal export to collectors.

Mandarin Duck (*Aix galericulata*)

- *IUCN Status:* least concern
- *Population trend:* decreasing.

The mandarin duck (the brightly coloured male is illustrated) may often be seen on ponds and lakes in Britain, but its native home is across eastern Asia, in Russia, China, Korea and Japan. It may be found on water which is near forests, but the forests are being felled and the water drained, making the duck more and more endangered.

Mountain Gorilla (*Gorilla beringei*)

- Subspecies beringei
- *IUCN Status:* critically Endangered
- *Population trend:* unknown
- *Population:* 300

The Virunga volcanoes region in eastern Zaire, Rwanda and Uganda is the only home of the highly endangered mountain gorilla. It depends on dense forests for survival and these are steadily being cut down to make way for crop growing and livestock grazing as well as mining. The gorilla is protected by law, but despite this, some of its so-called sanctuaries have been cleared, and hunters kill them for food and trophies, especially in the war-torn eastern Democratic Republic of Congo.

Jackass Penguin (*Spheniscus demersus*)

- *IUCN Status:* endangered
- *Population trend:* declining
- *Population:* 52,000 mature individuals

The jackass penguin is the only penguin to be found in Africa, and it was once the country's most common sea-bird. It lives off the coast of Namibia and South Africa, and the waters here have been over-fished by humans, depriving the birds of their food supply. Oil pollution also threatens them, as does the taking of their eggs for food.

Blue Whale (*Balaenoptera musculus*)

- *IUCN Status:* Endangered
- *Population trend:* increasing

An estimated 10,000-25,000 (3-11% of the 1911 population). (IUCN)

The largest animal ever to have lived on our planet, the blue whale, lives mainly in the cold waters of the Arctic and Antarctic, where it finds enough plankton to sustain it. It migrates to tropical seas to breed. The blue whale has been a protected species since 1966, but thousands were killed up until then. During the whaling season of 1930 to 1931 alone, 30,000 blue whales were killed by Antarctic whalers. It will take more than one hundred years of protection before we can be sure that it will not become extinct.

Numbat (*Myrmecobius fasciatus*)

- *IUCN Status:* Endangered
- *Population trend:* declining
- *Population:* under 1000

Sometimes called the banded anteater, the numbat was once common in the bush and forest of north-eastern and southern Australia. It is now only found in the most western part of eastern Australia. When man introduced predatory animals such as cats, dogs and foxes, these animals ate many numbats. Their numbers are still declining for the same reasons and also because their habitat is being cleared for farming and mining. Frequent fires destroy the logs which the animals use to shelter.

Komodo Dragon (*Varanus komodoensis*)

- *IUCN Status:* Vulnerable
- *Population trend:* stable (National Geographic)
- *Population:* 3,000-5,000 (National Geographic)

The Komodo dragon is the largest lizard in the world and lives on a few small Indonesian islands. It is a powerful predator and can measure as much as 3 metres in length. There are about 3,000 Komodo dragons in total, but they seem to be slowly declining. They live mainly on uninhabited islands, so are in no great danger from humans. Scientists think that natural causes are to blame. There are more males than females alive, and also the natural plant life seems to be changing and the lizards are not adapting well to their new environment.

Golden Lion Tamarin (*Leontopithecus rosalia*)

- *IUCN Status:* endangered

- *Population Trend:* stable
- *Population:* over 1000.

This tiny monkey is one of the most endangered of all animals in South America. The few that are left, are restricted to the only remaining coastal rainforest, southwest of Rio de Janeiro, Brazil. Forest destruction is the main reason for the tamarin's decline, but it is also in danger of being captured alive and sold as a pet - a strictly illegal practice which still goes on in secret. At their worst, numbers declined to as low as 250 but due to a captive breeding and reintroduction programme they have increased to a healthy 1000 and live in a protected area of forest. The problem they face now is that they do not have room to expand due to the fragmention of their habitat. Fires started by cattle farmers are a continued threat.

Spectacled Bear (*Tremarctos ornatus*)

- *IUCN Status:* Vulnerable
- *Population trend:* decreasing
- *Population:* no sufficient data; estimates of fewer than 3,000 (National Geographic)

This bear gets its name from a yellowish mask which makes it appear to be wearing a pair of spectacles! It lives in the forest-covered mountains of several South American countries. As the forests are cleared for farming, the bear's numbers fall. Even though it is protected by law, the spectacled bear is still killed by poachers for its fur, meat and fat.

Californian Condor (*Gymnogyps californianus*)

- *IUCN Status:* critically endangered
- *Population trend:* increasing
- *Population:* 104 adults, but currently only 44 are producing offspring.

During the nineteenth century this large bird of prey lived in the mountains of many areas of North America. It started to decline last century when it was killed by gold diggers who collected its long black feathers. Disturbance of its habitat by tourists, pesticides and low-flying aircraft also contributed to its downfall. In 1987 the last remaining wild Californian condors were taken into captivity. They have since been reintroduced to the wild with some success, but they are still at great risk.

Black-footed Ferret (*Mustela nigripes*)

- *IUCN Status:* endangered
- *Population trend:* increasing
- *Population:* 500 (breeding adults).

The black-footed ferret is America's rarest mammal. It was considered extinct in the wild in 1987 but through a captive breeding programme its numbers have risen. Its decline has been due to the decline of its primary prey. This ferret hunts prairie dogs on open grassland, and as this habitat has been turned into farmland, farmers have tried to eliminate the prairie dogs, viewed as a pest, by putting poison down their burrows. The black-footed ferret has also been poisoned by accident.

Our ancestors viewed the Earth as rich and bountiful, which it is. Many people in the past also saw nature as inexhaustibly sustainable, which we now know is the case only if we care for it. It is not difficult to forgive destruction in the past which resulted from ignorance. Today, however, we have access to more information, and it is essential that we re-examine ethically what we have inherited, what we are responsible for, and what we will pass on to coming generations. Our marvels of science and technology are matched if not outweighed by many current tragedies, including human starvation in some parts of the world, and the extinction of other life-forms. The exploration of space takes place at the same time as the Earth's own oceans, seas, and fresh water areas grow increasingly polluted. Many of the Earth's habitats, animals, plants, insects, and even micro-organisms that we know as rare may not be known at all by future generations. We have the capability, and the responsibility. We must act before it is too late."

White Rhinoceros

The White rhinoceros is one of the largest Northern subspecies ever to be described by scientists. This subspecies was classified in 1908. Today, it is very close to extinction in the wild, and few have ever been brought into captivity. The first captive White rhinos were received at the Antwerp Zoo, Belgium, in 1950. However, while they grew to maturity, these animals never bred. They have only bred at the Vychodoc'eska Zoo at Dvur Kralove in Czechoslovakia. The first southern white rhino that was ever born in captivity was born at Pretoria on June 8, 1967.

The most successful breeding of the White rhino in captivity has occurred in the San Diego Wild Animal Park. Seventy-five white Rhinos have been born as of 1988.

The white rhino is slightly larger than the black rhino with a larger head and body. They can weigh up to two tons and have a maximum age of up to fifty years. The horns of the rhino are the exact same substance as fingernails (keratin). The rhino is quite active and swift and can reach speeds of up to thirty m.p.h. This animal is surprisingly agile for its large size and can make sharp turns as it runs.

With a very acute sense of smell, it plays a large role in their social life. Mothers can identify their children or members of a particular 'home-range'. Their sense of smell also helps identify the territory of others. The female rhinoceros has a gestation period of fifteen-sixteen months, in which only one calf is born.

African Wild Asses

African Wild Asses are often referred to as the true asses and the domesticated ones we see today are believed to be descended from them. They are found scattered on the plains of Africa and travel in groups.

The asses are small, sturdy animals of from three to five feet at shoulder height. They are coloured from bluish grey to the colour fawn, with whitish muzzles and underparts. They are very swift runners and are able to inhabit acrid regions as they have become well adapted to suit the harsh deserts in which they live in.

The asses are very territorial. Stallions maintain areas under them and dominate over any of the other asses that come in their group. There is a very strong social bond between the females and the foals, where the foals are inseparable from their mothers the first few years of their lives.

The herds are formed when several asses come together casually.

These asses are endangered because of the interbreeding between them and other species and cause the wild asses descendants to become fewer and soon vanish. Illegal hunting and poaching for sport and body parts has also caused their rapid declination.

Leopards

Leopards are mainly found over nearly the whole of Africa, south of the Sahara, northeast and Asia. They are well known for their dark spots arranged in rosettes over much of their body without the central spot as found in jaguars.

Besides being known for their spots, they are also known for running very fast with up to speeds of about one hundred kilometres per hour. They also have the agility to climb trees as well as swim.

Their diet consist of antelope, wild pigs, monkeys, porcupines, birds and domestic livestock. They favour dogs as a meal. If they are unable to lure a dog out of the village, leopards are known to go right into the village to get the dog they want. They frequently store the remains of their kill up on trees for protection among the branches while they eat or rest.

In the past, leopards were considered a nuisance to cattle and were frequently shot or hunted. But as man destroyed their habitat for cattle, farming and other human activities, the leopards had no where to survive and their prey decreased due to immigration and lack of food. Therefore leopards had no choice but to kill cattle and domestic livestock. As a result, man killed them to protect their livestock. This caused the leopards to decrease drastically.

Besides that, the leopards were poached illegally for their valuable skin and body parts. In the 1980s and 1990s, the demand for their skins increased sharply due the furs' popularity in fashion.

Due the conservation efforts, these leopards are now a protected species in Uganda, Kenya, Ethiopia and most parts of the world. Efforts also have been made to hand breed them and then be released in the wild or enclosures are being made.

Gazelles

Gazelles are found in Africa and in Mongolia in Asia. They usually live in open plains and deserts. They are founds in herds of five to ten, but herds up to several hundred are found.

Gazelles are known for their graceful movements and alertness. Their colour consists of a shade of brown with white underparts and a horizontal black band running along each side of their body. Most species have horns on both of the sexes, with the horns often lyre-shaped. They run with a skip and have an amazing swiftness.

Gazelles are herbivores meaning they only eat plants. They forage among shrubs and short trees leaves. They are often hunted by other animals as a source of food. They use their swiftness to escape.

These graceful animals are endangered due the poaching for their skins and horns. Their habitats are also being destroyed by human development such as farming and cattling. Conservation efforts such as making their habitat area an enclosure for them and banning illegal poaching has helped a bit in their increase.

Giant Pandas

An estimated seven hundred Giant Pandas are left in the world today, living in the high mountains in coniferous forests and bamboo thickets in central China.

Since 1979 the San Diego Zoological Society has been working with Chinese zoos to spread the conservation message about the Chinese Giant Pandas. Before the Giant

Pandas were exported as State gifts, but now they are 'loaned' as 'conservation Pandas'. For example, two pandas visited for two hundred days in 1987 and 1988 at the San Diego Zoo and over two million people came and visited and enjoyed the Giant Pandas.

The Giant Pandas primary food source is bamboo. They eat it almost twelve hours a day and for the rest of the day they sleep. In the course of a year they eat almost 10,000 pounds of bamboo. However the giant panda routinely eats birds, snakes and bamboo rats. Giant Pandas live up to an age of 15 years in captivity and when one gives birth only one baby is born.

Once flourishing in the forests of Asia, there are now fewer than five thousand tigers left in the world. Already the Caspian and Malinese tigers are extinct. However, there finally is a law that bans hunting of tigers everywhere. Unfortunately there is even a greater threat to them which they face, a far greater threat than hunters.

Sumatran Tiger

Thousands of tigers have been killed in the last 50 years because their habitat has been destroyed by bulldozers and chainsaws. Already more than 80 per cent of India's forests have been destroyed. Still more forests are being cut down in order to sell firewood and lumber, plus to clear the land for farming.

Despite all of the hardships and disasters that this animal has endured, the tiger population has actually risen over the last ten years. This has only been possible through strict laws protecting these magnificent animals and wilderness preserves around the world. However, this is just a small step in saving the tigers. New preserves must be added, but finding these preserves will not be easy. There must be enough water, prey, and plants for their prey to feed on. The people living near the tigers must manage and control the commercial use of the lands natural resources.

The Komodo Dragon

The Komodo Dragon is the largest living lizard on earth. Discovered in 1912 on small islands in Indonesia, this lizard can weigh over 350 pounds and grow over 10 feet long.

There are several differences between the female and the male Komodo Dragons. The female is an olive-brown colour with yellow patches on her throat. She has an incubation period of 6-8 weeks and can lay up to 25 eggs. All Komodo Dragons reach a sexual maturity at the age of 3-5 years and live over the age of 25. Male dragons are a lot larger and vary in colour from a dark grey to a brick red.

These reptiles are the largest predators on the islands in which they live. They hunt hog-deer, wild pig, macaques, rats, and dig up eggs of mound birds (the mound birds eggs are considered a free treat whenever a Komodo Dragon crosses their path). When they eat, the dragons take a huge chunk of flesh of the preys' body. Using their forefeet to hold down the prey, the Komodo Dragon then swallows the flesh without chewing. Komodo Dragons use their eyes to locate prey and find it extremely difficult to see stationary animals. They have a rudimentary sense of hearing and a fairly acute sense of smell.

When they are born Komodo Dragons are left to fend for themselves. Sometimes their parents can forget they are their children and eat them. Up until the age of about 2-3 years old they are able to climb up trees and stay there. Climbing protects them from the predators on the ground and they capture prey by jumping down and landing on their unsuspecting backs. This sudden attack is one of the only ways a young dragon can survive, the other way is their surprising speed. Even a full grown lizard can run up to 35 miles per hour.

When the Komodo Dragons eats, there is a strict order of priority feeding enforced by the males. The strongest male will eat first and not let any others eat until he has had his share. However females are allowed to eat without any interference and can tolerate each others presence.

The Komodo Dragon makes a burrow about 3-6 feet wide in the ground and can be active both in the day and the night. In the night they use their tongue to find their way in the dark, for it has an extremely sensitive sense of taste and scent stimuli.

Male Komodo Dragons are territorial. During there mating period they engage in 'boxing matches' with each other. However they do not use their claws, teeth or their strong, powerful tail.

Tapirs

Tapirs are found in small groups in the tropical rain forests of Malaysia and Central America. They are short-legged and heavy-bodied with small eyes, rounded ears and small trunks protruding over their mouths. Their body hair are often short and usually sparse. The main source of food is grass and shrubs as well as certain roots.

The central American tapirs are plain grey or brown in colour, but the Malaysian tapirs have a distinct black and white pattern. The heads, shoulders and legs are black while the rumps, backs and bellies are white. The young are completely different from their parents, with a dark brown colour and streaked as well as spotted with yellowish white.

Tapirs are shy and often travel near water. When they are disturbed, they will crash wildly through the undergrowth and hide in the water.

Tapirs are easy prey as they do not run fast and do not have special defences, therefore easily become victims to carnivorous animals and hunters. Their habitat, the rain forests are also depleting quickly destroyed by human activities, leading even more to their decline.

The Seladang

The seladang or otherwise known as gaur or forest buffalo are found in India, Burma and Malaysia. Their build is larger than any other wild cattle with shoulder heights of up to six feet or more. They are heavy bodied with a high ridge on the forepart of the back and possess curved horns on their heads and white stockinged feet.

The bulls are dark brown or blackish in colour while the cows and the young are reddish brown.

They used to be found throughout the country but are now found in scattered herds in certain parts of the area. This is due to the deforestation of their habitat by man. They are also hunted for their meat and for sport.

The Bird of Paradise

The bird of paradise is noted for its vibrant colours and bizarre shapes of the male birds' plumage during the mating season. They are found in the New Guinea highlands and islands and some are also found in Australia.

The males' colourful plumage is used to attract females during their breeding season. The females are dull brown with scattered brown specks. Courting males will strut around on a chosen perch or a cleared spacing on the forest floor for hours, showing off their magnificent feathers of different shapes and sizes. After mating, the females will go off and make a nest on their own, taking care of the young unaided.

Some birds of paradise have extra long tail and flank feathers trailing behind as they fly while some are adorned with colourful feathers around the neck which can be erected to form ruffs.

Naturally, when explorers from other countries came to the land, the brightly coloured birds caught their attention. A few were brought back to their homeland and the Bird of Paradise feathers soon became a fashion statement. By the nineteenth century, popular demand of the feathers had made the number of birds decline rapidly and almost caused extinction. Fortunately, conservation efforts managed to save the species before they were wiped out but the number of surviving birds are still small even today due to illegal poaching in their habitat.

Leatherback Turtles

Leatherback Turtles are found in most warm seas, often migrating from one continent to another. They are the largest of all turtles, sometimes weighing more than 1500 pounds.

Their shells are covered by a thick layer of smooth leathery skin, instead of scales. Unlike other turtles, their ribs and backbones are not joined to the shell. These turtles have huge strong front flippers which can propel them in the water at high speeds.

Leatherback Turtles have a very unique way of laying their eggs. From August to September, female turtles travel vast distances just to lay their eggs on the exact spot where they had laid their eggs previously. Without fail, their homing instincts are always right and rarely do they lose their way to their nesting site. As soon as they reach the shore, they will not rest until they have arrived at their nesting grounds. By using their giant flippers, they heave themselves up towards the spot and dig a deep hole in the sand. In this hole, they will lay about 100 to 200 soft rubbery eggs at one time. While they are laying the eggs, they will start shedding tears to excrete the excess salt from their bodies while swimming in the sea water. Once they are finished, the turtles will cover up the hole with sand and return to the sea, only coming next year to the same spot to dig another hole to lay eggs.

The heat of the sun will warm the eggs and after a period of time, the hatchlings will climb out of the sand and crawl towards the sea. Even though many turtles are hatched, many do not survive the first few weeks of their lives. There are many predators such as seagulls who prey on the young turtles. The baby turtle's hard shell has not yet formed and has no hardened defence against the attackers. Some turtles are caught in fishermen's nets and left out to die. Other turtles are caught between the wastes man created such as plastic bags and eventually die of suffocation and strangulation.

To make matters worse, Leatherback Turtles are hunted for their ornamental shell while their eggs are considered delicacies. Illegal gathering for eggs to be sold in markets also helps in the decline of these turtles.

The coming ashore of the Leatherback Turtles to lay their eggs have become quite a spectacle and have drawn large crowds to witness this event. Unfortunately, the crowds created a large amount of noise and drove many turtles away. They also made campfires which scared them away.

In order to protect them, the Malaysian government has declared it as a protected animal. Various rules and regulations have been made and huge fines imposed on those who break the law.

The Japanese Ibis

The Japanese Ibis has a white body with a red face. They often wade in shallow lagoons, bays and marshes. They use their long slightly curved bills to pick up any small fish and soft molluscs while wading.

While they fly, their neck and legs are stretched out. They fly by alternately flapping and sailing through the air. Their nests are of compact size made out of sticks found in the branches of trees or bushes.

These birds are considered to be on the verge of extinction and the Japanese government has build different programmes to increase the species such as breeding them in captivity.

The Japanese Ibis is endangered due to the excessive hunting of the birds and the destruction of their habitat by man. They also face food problems as more of their feeding land is used up for human activities.

Bald Eagle

Since the first census records were kept of the Bald Eagle, the national bird of the U.S., in the 1800s there has been a continuous decline in their population. Bald Eagles were endangered in 43 states and threatened in five. However, the Bald Eagle was relatively abundant only in Alaskan and Canadian wilderness areas. Historically, Bald Eagles had been observed in all of the United States except Hawaii.

Man is the Bald Eagle's main enemy and predator. During migration, breeding, and winter periods the Bald Eagle requires a large home range area, leaving itself vulnerable to habitat destruction by man. Also environmental problems have decreased the population of bald eagles. The most serious ones are pollution by pesticides and heavy metals that contaminate streams and fish, in turn stopping the Bald Eagle's food chain.

During the 1940s, the number of hatched eaglets recorded by field biologists rapidly declined. This was because of a fatal eggshell thinning that was the result from exposure to DDE a metabolic by product of DDT which is a organochlorinated pesticide. The eagles received this pesticide mainly through the fish they ate because the rivers were contaminated by the poison.

In nationwide autopsies of dead birds collected by federal, state, and private cooperators, federal government pathologists routinely found DDT, DDE, dieldrin, polychlorinated biphenyls (PCBs), and other pesticide and insecticide residues in Bald Eagle carcasses. Because of all the pesticides that killed these magnificent birds in the 1960's the Bald Eagle was named America's most polluted Bird. A nation wide ban was made on the use of DDT, there was an increase in wildlife protection and rehabilitation efforts, more field studies and a captive programme that have aided in the recovery of this species.

The National Wildlife Federation and the National Audubon Society have mounted publicity campaigns to inform the public about the sad history of the bald eagle. Federal and state wildlife and game officials have also been leaders in establishing bald eagle future recovery plans and management. The San Diego Zoo and other zoos nation wide continue to aid the efforts to preserve this species.

The California Condor

The California Condor is one of the rarest of all North American birds and one of the rarest birds in the world. In fact, during the first half of the century there were only 60 individual condors. Now there is less than 40 despite the conservation efforts that are put forth by biologists and other American authorities. Today the California Condor's range is limited to a small region that is north of Los Angeles. Soaring at speeds of 35-40 miles per hour the California Condor cleaned carrion from roads, ranches and beaches. There is absolutely no record of these magnificent birds attacking a living animal, however they were routinely shot, mostly by farmers and ranchers. Also California Condors were being exterminated by lead poisoning. However, zoologists are trying to change the condor's upcoming fate. Molloko is the first ever captive condor that was bred in captivity in history, born in April, 1988 at the San Diego Wild Animal Park. Its future lies in the hands of captive breeding and when it gets older, reintroduction to the wild. Hopefully Molloko's story will help educate the public.

The California Condor is about 3-4 feet in length and varies in weight from 20-30 pounds. The California condor has a huge wingspan which is about 9-10 and a half feet. When nesting they nest in cracks of rocks and lay only one egg.

This bird's plumage is black with a tint of blue metallic reflections. It has white bars underneath its wing.

Polar Bears

Polar Bears are found throughout the arctic region, often covering hundreds of miles in their range. They have heavy white fur which camouflage them against the white landscape in which they live in.

Despite their size, they are extremely fast runners and wide-ranging travellers. They are also expert swimmers, with their thick layer of fur and fat insulating them against the extreme cold of their climate. They have hairy soles on their broad feet to protect them and insulate them from the cold, as well as help them move across the snow swiftly.

Their diet consists of fish, seal, caribou, birds, seaweed, grass and an occasional whale which strayed too far from its course.

Polar Bears are usually shy but they are known to be dangerous when attacked or confronted. They give birth to one to four cubs at a time in the winter and the cubs stay with their mother for up to three years.

Polar Bears are endangered due to the man's excessive hunting for their priceless hide, tendons, meat, fat and flesh. Their numbers dwindled from several hundred thousands to a few hundred in a few years time. In efforts to protect Polar Bears, an international agreement was set up in 1973 whereby only traditional weapons were allowed to be used in the hunting of the Polar Bears.

Peregrine Falcons

Peregrine Falcons are birds of prey which were once found worldwide but are now rare almost everywhere.

They are strong and fast and fly to tremendous speeds. They are able to dive and clench their victims with their strong talons and kill them on impact. In the 18th and the 19th century, man captured and trained these falcons as hunting weapons to kill small prey.

They nest in between rock edges high on cliffs and usually near water where prey are plentiful. Their food consists of smaller birds, ducks and fish. They lay one to four eggs at a time.

The numbers of Peregrine Falcons have dwindled due to the poisonous chemicals such as DDT found in their food chain. Their food, for example fish, consume poisonous substances in their food and these fish are contaminated. In turn, the fish are eaten by the falcons and the poisonous substances are passed down to the falcon's body. These chemicals interfere with the reproductive organs and cause the shells of their eggs to become thin and brittle. These eggs are easily broken when the parents sit on them and the eggs are destroyed. As a result, less and less peregrines falcons are hatched.

Another factor that causes the Peregrine Falcon's endangerment is the destruction of their habitat by human activities. Theyare also hunted for sport. In efforts to increase their population, steps to hand breed and release them into areas where they have become extinct have been undertaken. But the ultimate step to conserve them is by elimating all chemical substances from their food source.

Ibexes

Ibexes are wild goats found on high mountain meadows, slopes and rocks of Europe, northeastern Africa and Asia.

Their forelegs are slighter shorter than hind legs with a height of 3 feet at the shoulder. Both sexes have horns which curve backwards from the forehead. During the winter, their fur is yellowish brown while in the summer their fur turns to ashy grey.

Ibexes live apart in small flocks most of the time but during mating season they will pair off. They are extremely agile, able to survive in cliffs and crags. They are known to leap up to lengths as far as 40 feet. They are herbivores and eat whatever green vegetation is found in their sparse landscape.

Ibexes have become endangered because of the excessive hunting by man for game and sport. Hunters consider it a feat to be able to reach the inaccessible habitat in which they live in and kill the Ibexes as 'souvenirs'.

The Alpine Ibex has become very rare and are protected under the Italian government. They have been introduced to various parts of the world suitable for their living to increase their numbers.

Musk Oxen

Musk Oxen are roaming in parts of Europe, northern Canada and Greenland. They are stocky with large heads, short necks and legs. They are extremely huge in size with a bull weighing up to about 880 pounds. Both male and female have horns which can reach up to 2 feet as found in old males. They have long shaggy brown hair that cover the whole body that reach nearly up to their feet and conceal a short tail. Their face is further covered by short hair.

Underneath their shaggy hair, they have a thick layer of wool which they shed during the summer. This wool will be collected by the Eskimos to be made into fine cloth, resembling cashmere.

Musk Oxen travel in herds of 20 to 30. When attacked, the adults will form a circle with the young safe inside. The adults will face the outside and use their sharp horns as weapons against their enemy. The predator attacks young oxen who stray too far from their herd when they attack.

Musk Oxen have become endangered due to the excessive hunting by man for food and sport. Their habitat also have been destroyed by human activities.

Takahe

The Takahe is a rare flightless bird found only in New Zealand. It was thought to be extinct in the 1800's but was rediscovered 1948 in several remote valleys on South Island.

It has a plumage of brilliant blue and copper-green with large red bill and a red frontal shield that protrudes out from its head. It feeds by stripping seeds from grasses. It nests on the ground and lays two cream coloured eggs with black blotches. The young are black in colour with downy feathers.

Takahes are endangered because:

- their habitat has been destroyed for agriculture and construction of buildings, roads, and dams;
- when New Zealand was first discovered by explorers, they brought in many other kinds of animals and these animals hunted the Takahe. The Takahe, being flightless and unable to fly away when in danger was quickly destroyed, just like the Dodo bird.

Koalas

Koalas are found in the coastal regions of Eastern Australia. It is a marsupial mammal that gives birth to underdeveloped young and the young are carried around in their mother's pouch.

Koalas have strong clawed feet and are able to grip the branches firmly. They are extremely fussy eaters and only feed very selectively on eucalyptus leaves. To aid in the digestion of these leaves, Koalas have a long caecum and extra long intestines.

Koalas have only one young at a time and their young remains in their mother's pouch for up to 7 months. When it is 1 year old, baby Koalas cling to their mother's back constantly.

Koalas have become endangered because:

- it is valued for its soft fur.
- if a disease is spread among them, they have no resistance against it because of them having the same genetic pool. Therefore they are not immune to disease and if one Koala gets a virus, the whole community is infected by it as well. Often these diseases bring disastrous results and hundreds or thousands or maybe even millions can be wiped out because of a single virus.
- their habitat is being destroyed. Besides having no living place, it has lost its source of food. As the Koala is an very fussy eater and almost only eats eucalyptus leaves, it has a limited supply of food choice.

The Scarlet Macaw

The Scarlet Macaw is found in the treetops from Mexico to southern Brazil. It is about 90 centimetres in length and is bright red with blue and yellow wings, blue and red tail which is a unique feature in the family and a white face with big, sickle-shaped beaks. Its feet are able to grasp the limbs of a tree very firmly. When a Macaw is fully developed, the tail is more than two feet long. Both the male and females look alike. It is the among the most well known among the species.

It feeds on the abundant fruits and nuts found in the tropical forests which is its habitat. It cracks open the nuts by using its extremely powerful beak and uses its blunt tongue to extract the nut meat. It also uses its beak to cut out pieces of fruit. Occasionally it eats insects and worms.

Macaw do not have feathers on its face and sometimes blushes when excited or angry. It usually travels in a large flock. It is easily tamed and its life span is about 50 to 60 years. It builds its nest in holes in trees or in crevices between rocks. The young hatch in about 3 weeks and are cared for by both the parents for 2 to 3 months.

Scarlet Macaws are famous for its ability in mimicking and imitating sounds made by the human voice as well as perform tricks.

This bird has become endangered due to the overwhelming demand for its colourful feathers in fashion in earlier centuries. Demand has not diminished until now as the young are taken from their nests for pets by poachers. This has led to a great decline to the Scarlet Macaw's population.

Law enforcement has been made in most of the countries where the Scarlet Macaw is found, but heavier penalties are yet to be enforced.

The Quetzal

The Quetzal, one of best known species from the trogon family, it was a sacred bird of the ancient Mayas and the Aztecs. Its feathers were used in the clothing of their priests and royal family. Instead of killing them to acquire the feathers, the feathers were plucked from the bird as it was considered a crime which was punishable by death to kill a Quetzal. Today, it is the national emblem of Guatemala.

The Quetzal is found in South Mexico to Bolivia in the hot lowland of the tropics but some are found in the mountains. The whole body is about 50 inches in length. The tail is covered by extra long blue-green plumes. When it flies, the tail shows white underneath. The head has a rounded hair-like crest and its breast is gold-green while the belly is red. Its back is blue with curly gold-tinged mantle.

It nests in holes in trees, at times a natural cavity in a tree. Both the parents share in the duty of caring for their young.

The Quetzal was hunted for its magnificent feathers when the continent was explored by the explorers that arrived and still is. The colourful feathers are used in the fashion trade and fetch very high prices. Due to this, poaching of these birds has greatly affected its population. The destruction of its habitat the forests for construction too has depleted their numbers.

The Vicuna

The Vicuna lives high in the Andes mountains of Peru, Bolivia, Argentina and Chile. It belongs to the camel family and is a close relative of the llama. It is a small, slender animal with orange red fur and big ears and eyes.

The Vicuna generally roams the mountains in small herds. It has never been fully domesticated by man.

Vicunaa are hunted for their hides and wool which are valued for weaving fabrics clothes and garments. As a result, the numbers of the Vicuna have depleted due to the over-poaching. The fabric made from the fur is also called vicuna.

The Giant Anteater

The Giant Anteater lives in forests, swampy areas and open plains of Mexico, Central America and South America. It walks and roams around in densely populated areas during the night.

It eats insects and picks its prey up by rapidly flicking its long sticky tongue in and out. Its mouth is long and tubular and does not have any teeth. Of all the anteaters, it is the largest species and can weigh up to 39 kg or 86 lbs. Its body is covered with a coarse coat with a gray stripe running down each shoulder. Its tail is long and bushy. It has long front claws which is used for defense against enemies and tearing apart termite mounds. Their claws are so long that they are tucked under its feet and the anteater walks on its knuckles.

It is a solitary animal and gives birth to only one young. It carries the young on its back for almost a year during its growth.

The Giant Anteater's numbers have depleted due to the loss of its habitat to human construction. The fact that its reproduction rate is very low does not encourage the increase of its numbers.

The Bespectacled Bear

The Bespectacled Bear is found from Bolivia to Colombia, being restricted to high, steep and rugged areas unsuitable for agriculture.

It is mostly brown or black with white, cream or orange shading around the chest, neck and a ring encircling each eye. It is relatively small with the males weighing about 80 kg and the females about 60 kg. Each foot has five sharp, short and powerful claws which are used for climbing and tearing apart trees.

It feeds on wild fruits, especially figs, leaves, small animals, insects, herbs and grasses. It spends much of its time on top of trees and builds a nest every night. It is very vocal as it makes trilling noises as it travels around and the young hum when they are relaxed.

Although it is not a threat to humans, the Bespectacled Bear is killed as it does damage to agriculture. It is also killed for its meat. As a result, the number of Bespectacled Bears is dwindling. Only in Bolivia is their situation somewhat secure, but no one knows how long that security will last.

Beginning of Life

Life began on our planet about 3,500 million years ago. The first living things were found in the sea, and over the course of millions of years, from these early life forms, a rich variety of animals has descended. Through the process we call evolution, animals have become adapted to enable them to live in all parts of the world, sometimes in the most hostile environments.

Almost 600 million years ago, the invertebrates appeared i.e. those animals without backbones - insects and other minibeasts. The earliest vertebrates i.e. animals with backbones, were in the form of primitive fish and appeared around 500 million years ago. From these, all the other fishes descended, as well as amphibians, reptiles, birds and mammals.

The animal kingdom is enormous and we do not know for certain how many species there are in the world. Around 1.5 million species of animal have been named and described by scientists - and over a million of these are insects. It is known that there are about twice as many animals in tropical rainforests than in any other habitat, and it is here that there are likely to be countless numbers of species yet unknown to science. It has been estimated that the total number of insect species alone could be around 30 million!

It is just possible, but unlikely, that there are a few large animals remaining to be discovered, but what we can be sure of is that the most numerous large animal on Earth is Homo sapiens - the human! Modern man appeared about 30,000 years ago and has increasingly come to dominate the planet. The steady increase in population was speeded up by advances in civilization such as the Industrial Revolution and better health and medical care.

The rate in increase of the human population is slowing down in parts of the Northern Hemisphere, but it continues to rise in Third World countries, despite the effect of famine, floods, disease and war. Allowing for the deathrate, over one million more humans come into the world each week!

This population explosion means that millions of people suffer from hunger and disease, and more and more wild places are taken over, causing animals and plants to suffer too.

Extinction is for ever!

As almost everyone knows, to become extinct is to be gone forever. Even before human's arrival on Earth, species became extinct quite naturally. Natural extinction happens when a species declines in numbers gradually but steadily at the end of its evolutionary period on Earth. The length of this period depends on how well a species can adapt to changes in climate and changes in other animals and plants around it. This process of extinction can take a very long time - sometimes several million years - and the extinction of one species is immediately followed by the appearance of another in a continuous cycle.

The case of the dinosaurs is the most well-known example of natural extinction. These reptiles appeared on Earth about 200 million years ago and dominated both land and sea for almost 100 million years. It is not certain why the dinosaurs became extinct, but their disappearance was a natural one and new species of animals evolved to replace them.

The rate of extinction has speeded up unnaturally over the last 400 years, rising sharply since 1900. This increase in the rate of extinction is directly related to the increase in the human population over the same period of time. The vast number of humans has caused great damage to the planet, as wild habitats have been taken over, forcing animals and plants into smaller and smaller areas, until some of them have become extinct. We have also polluted some habitats with chemicals and refuse, making them unfit for wildlife. These causes of extinction are known as indirect destruction.

Animals may also become extinct through direct destruction. This includes the hunting and capturing of animals. Humans have always hunted and killed wildlife but early humans lived more in harmony with nature, they killed animals for essentials like food and clothing. When guns were invented mass destruction of species was possible. Animals have been, and still are, killed for meat, clothing,medicines, feathers, eggs, trophies, tourist souvenirs - and sometimes just for amusement. Some species are still captured in the wild for the live pet trade, even though their numbers are dwindling.

The extinction of at least 500 species of animals has been caused by man, most of them in this century. Today there are about 5,000 endangered animals and at least one species dies out every year. There are probably many more which become extinct without anyone knowing.

The main threats to species then can be cited as poaching, habitat loss and climate change. The International Union for Conservation of Nature has its own 'red list' of endangered species ranging from 'least concern' through to 'critically endangered'. It is their assessment which we'll refer to here.

The dodo has become a symbol of extinction. It was a turkey-sized flightless pigeon which lived on the island of Mauritius. When sailors landed on the island for the first time in the sixteenth century, they killed the helpless bird for food. The dodo's eggs and young were eaten by dogs, cats, pigs, rats and monkeys which man had introduced to the island. The dodo, unused to predators, very quickly declined in numbers - and it was extinct by 1681.

Is it Important to Save Animals From Extinction?

Some people may ask 'why bother with conservation?' We now realise that it is important to maintain the planet's biodiversity, that it is the richness (variety) of animal and plant life, its abundance and wild habitats. The more species disappear, the more entire eco-systems become vulnerable and would eventually fall apart as the links in the food chains become broken. For example certain animals only eat certain plants and those plants may need that animal to pollinate it or spread its seed. Without one, the other is also likely to die out.

From a selfish point of view, we humans never know how valuable a species of animal or plant may be for us in the future, perhaps as food, medicines (particularly plants) or specific information.

Saving Endangered Animals

People all over the world are working to help save endangered animals from extinction. There are conservation organisations which try to make people aware of the problems facing wild animals. Some of the ways in which they are being saved include habitat protection, captive breeding, setting up nature reserves and parks and using alternative products in place of products from rare animals.

Governments can help by making international agreements between countries to protects animals (many countries, for example, have agreed to stop hunting the blue whale) and their habitats. There has been agreement from a number of countries in June 2010 to protect the rainforests and prevent deforestation through financial backing.

Scientists are setting up gene banks in which they keep an animal's genetic material (the 'building blocks' of a living thing) in suspended animation. This technique may make it possible in the future to 'grow' a new animal of the same species. Kew Gardens, London has a seed bank in case plant species become extinct in the wild.

The first step towards saving animals is to learn as much as possible about them. If we know where and how they live, and what they need to survive, then it will be easier to help them. It is also a good idea to learn from our mistakes of the past, such as destroying too much rainforest and over-hunting animals. To ensure the survival of the world's animals we must learn how to keep 'sustainable populations' alive i.e. populations with enough numbers for the animals to survive on their own. The dodo and all the other which man has made extinct became so because their populations fell below a sustainable level. It is worth keeping in mind that those animals may well become the endangered animals of tomorrow.

CHAPTER

Wildlife Conservation

A tree is often the symbol used to represent the environmental movement. In fact, we adopted the colour green, the plant's colour, as the main adjective to define general environmentalism. Why is the forest such an important element for the environment? There are many reasons why we benefit from forests and there are obviously many consequences that stem from the loss of 13 million hectares of forest every year.

Forests Stabilize the Climate

Forests stabilize the climate in general. The plants enrich the soil by recycling the nutrients through the shedding of leaves and seeds. They also regulate the water cycle by absorbing and redistributing rainwater quite equally to every species living within its range, which is known as the economy of water. Overall, forests provide perfect habitats for life to flourish on land. They actually contain most of the living species, particularly in the case of tropical forests where up to 90 per cent of the planet's species live. Tropical forests possess the highest level of biodiversity and therefore provide the biggest genes reservoir.

Plants also play a crucial role in the purification of our air. When breathing, they absorb carbon dioxide and release oxygen. They were the reason why life outside of water became possible in the first place. We find in them a powerful tool to fight air pollution and consequently, global warming.

Finally, forests provide us with a huge amount of different medicine material. Important amounts of the drugs we use are extracted from tropical plants and animals and the majority of drugs used to fight cancer are coming from there as well. Forests contain a potential source of an amazing amount of cures, but most of it hasn't been discovered yet. Human health is directly linked with the conservation of forests and all of their aspects.

Deforestation has been going on for centuries and is intimately correlated with population growth. Besides colonisation, we cut trees for practically the same reasons as hundreds of years ago: to increase land for agriculture and pasture, as well as to produce lumber for heating, construction and other material. For agriculture and pasture, burning the area is often used to flatten the ground, which emits an important amount of carbon dioxide each time. We also create big industrial projects such as artificial water basins to produce hydro electricity. Industrial development has often been responsible for deforestation, and has threatened in some cases the ways of life of certain populations.

By eliminating forests, we kill most of the biodiversity in the area. In some places in tropical forests that means it would take another 100 millions years to recreate the same biodiversity; some of the species are unique in the world and they quickly disappear following the destruction of their habitat. Deforestation provokes irreversible damage and reforestation is not entirely making it up for it.

Other consequences such as soil impoverishment are related to the clear cutting of forests. Once a forest is not there to absorb the water from the rain, this creates floods and provokes soil erosion. Most of the nutrients and the elements needed to maintain life are then washed away. In the tropics, deforestation can lead to desertification, where the area becomes a desert and loses most of its life.

Taking this problem to an economic level, agriculture, pasture and logging are common activities today, especially in the Third World. Expanding these activities often leads to deforestation. For a long time, international banks provided loans to unindustrialized countries in order to create development and prosperity. Unfortunately, large interests took control, and the way they chose to repay it rapidly was to exploit forests, creating only short term profit.

In the longer term, their overexploitations lead to the destruction of forests and the impoverishment of the people. They lost a very important resource and hardly gained anything in terms of development. Countries like Ethiopia have destroyed 98 per cent of their forests to satisfy immediate needs. In less than 100 years, they've gone from 40 per cent of the land being covered by forests to only 1 per cent. Yet they haven't made considerable improvements in development. The most devastating deforestation has been made to create short term profits.

Most countries don't have proper regulations and the exploitation of forests has been quite anarchic. If we continue at this rhythm, we will lose all tropical forests before 2100. But there is a way to ethically exploit our forests.

We can find many exploitable natural products without clear cutting the area. For example, rubber is a product extracted from the tropical forest and does not require clearing up the area, which shows that the exploitation can be done in a sustainable way. Techniques like these have been massively promoted in recent years in order to save the unique Amazonian forest. What we have left in the world is crucial to maintain biodiversity, find new medicine and absorb air pollution. Those things are unconditionally linked to human survival.

Wildlife Conservation

Wildlife conservation is the wise use, regulation, and restoration of wildlife and their habitats, especially in relation to endangered and vulnerable species. All living non-domesticated animals, even if bred, hatched or born in captivity, are considered wild animals. Wildlife represents all the non-cultivated and non-domesticated animals living in their natural habitats. Our world has many unique and rare mammals, birds and reptiles. However the pressure of growing population in different parts of the world has led to the increasing need of using land for human habitations and agriculture. This has led to the reduced habitat of many wild animals.

Major Threats to Wildlife

Major threats to wildlife can be categorized as below:

- **Habitat loss**: Fewer natural wildlife habitat areas remain each year. Moreover, the habitat that remains has often been degraded to bear little resemblance to the natural wild areas which existed in the past.
- **Climate change**: Because many types of plants and animals have specific habitat requirements, climate change could cause disastrous loss of wildlife species. A slight drop or rise in average rainfall will translate into large seasonal changes. Hibernating mammals, reptiles, amphibians and insects are harmed and disturbed. Plants and wildlife are sensitive to moisture change so, they will be harmed by any change in the moisture level.
- **Pesticides and toxic chemicals**: Pesticides are deliberately spread to make the environment toxic to certain plants, insects, and rodents, so it should not be surprising that other plants and wildlife are deliberately harmed at the same time. In addition many chemical pollutants are toxic to wildlife, such as PCBs, mercury, petroleum by-products, solvents, antifreeze, etc.
- **Unregulated Hunting and poaching**: Unregulated hunting and poaching causes a major threat to wildlife. Along with this, mismanagement of forest department and forest guards triggers this problem.
- **Natural phenomena**: Floods, earthquakes, volcanoes, lightning, forest fires.
- **Pollution**: Pollutants released into the environment are ingested by a wide variety of organisms.

- **Over-exploitation of resources**: Exploitation of wild populations for food has resulted in population crashes (over-fishing, for example).
- **Accidental deaths**: Car hits, window collisions (birds), collisions with ships (whales).

The North American Model of Wildlife Conservation is considered to be one the most successful conservation model in world. It has its origins in 19th century conservation movements, the near extinction of several species of wildlife (including the American Bison) and the rise of sportsmen with the middle class. Beginning in the 1860s sportsmen began to organize and advocate for the preservation of wilderness areas and wildlife. The North American Model of Wildlife Conservation rests on two basic principles – fish and wildlife are for the non-commercial use of citizens, and should be managed such that they are available at optimum population levels forever. These core principles are elaborated upon in the seven major tenets of the model.

In the North American Model, wildlife is held in the public trust. This means that fish and wildlife are held by the public through state and federal governments. In other words, though an individual may own the land up which wildlife resides, that individual does not own said wildlife. Instead, the wildlife is owned by all citizens. With origins in Roman times and English Common law, the public trust doctrine has at its heart the 1842 Supreme Court ruling.

Under the North American Model, wildlife exist outside the market, removing any direct commercial value from wild game as they and the meat thereof cannot be bought or sold. Certain products such as antlers and fur may, however, be bought and sold. The end of market hunting was a major step in the restoration of North American species. By removing the pressure of market hunting allowed game and fish species to recover and eventually be taken by hunters and anglers at sustainable levels.

Hunting and Angling Laws are Created Through the Public Process

Through democratic representation, citizens create the policies that regulate, conserve, and manage wildlife within the United States and Canada. The creation and implementation of wildlife and natural resource management policy is an open and public process.

All citizens have a right to hunting and fishing. Additionally the management of fish and wildlife is funded through the sale of licenses and in the taxation of hunting and fishing equipment. Additional funding comes from state and federal budgets, but the bulk of funding is through these sources.

Under the North American Model, the killing of game must be done only for food, fur, self-defense, and the protection of property (including livestock). In other words, it is broadly regarded as unlawful and unethical to kill fish or wildlife (even with a license) without making all reasonable effort to retrieve and make reasonable use of the resource.

Wildlife as an International Resource

As wildlife do exist only within fixed political boundaries, effective management of these resources must be done internationally, through treaties and the cooperation of management agencies.

Scientific Management of Wildlife

Effective management of wildlife and other natural resources must be based on continuous and sound scientific research.

The Wildlife Conservation Act was enacted by the Government of India in 1972. Soon after the trend of policy makers enacting regulations on conservation a strategy was developed to allow actors, both government and non-government, to follow a detailed "framework" to successful conservation. The World Conservation Strategy was developed in 1980 by the "International Union for Conservation of Nature and Natural Resources (IUCN) with advice, cooperation and financial assistance of the United Nations Environment Programme (UNEP) and the World Wildlife Fund and in collaboration with the Food and Agriculture Organisation of the United Nations (FAO) and the United Nations Educational, Scientific and Cultural Organisation (Unesco)" The strategy aims to "provide an intellectual framework and practical guidance for conservation actions." This thorough guidebook covers everything from the intended 'users' of the strategy to its very priorities and even a map section containing areas that have large seafood consumption therefore endangering the area to over fishing. The main sections are as follows:

The objectives of conservation and requirements for their achievement:

- Maintenance of essential ecological processes and life-support systems.
- Preservation of genetic diversity.
- Sustainable utilization of species and ecosystems.
- Priorities for national action.
- A framework for national and subnational conservation strategies.
- Policy making and the integration of conservation and development.
- Environmental planning and rational use allocation.
- Priorities for international action:
- International action: law and assistance.
- Tropical forests and drylands.
- A global programme for the protection of genetic resource areas.
- Map sections.
- Tropical forests.
- Deserts and areas subject to desertification.

As 'major development agencies' became 'discouraged with the public sector' of environmental conservation in the late 1980s, these agencies began to lean their support towards the 'private sector' or non-government organisations (NGOs). In a World Bank Discussion Paper it is made apparent that "the explosive emergence of nongovernmental organisations" was widely known to government policy makers. Seeing this rise in NGO support, the U.S. Congress made amendments to the Foreign Assistance Act in 1979 and 1986 "earmarking U.S. Agency for International Development (USAID) funds for biodiversity". From 1990 moving through recent years environmental conservation in the NGO sector has become increasingly more focused on the political and economic impact of USAID given towards the 'Environment and Natural Resources'. After the terror attacks on the World Trade Centers on September 11, 2001 and the start of former President Bush's War on Terror, maintaining and improving the quality of the environment and natural resources became a 'priority' to 'prevent international tensions' according to the Legislation on Foreign Relations Through 2002 and section 117 of the 1961 Foreign Assistance Act. Furthermore in 2002 U.S. Congress modified the section on endangered species of the previously amended Foreign Assistance Act.

The amendments to the section also included modifications on the section concerning 'PVOs and other Non-governmental Organisations'. The section requires that PVOs and NGOs "to the fullest extent possible involve local people with all stages of design and implementation." These amendments to the Foreign Assistance Act and the recent rise in USAID funding towards foreign environmental conservation have led to several disagreements in terms of NGOs' role in foreign development.

World Wide Fund for Nature (WWF) is an international non-governmental organisation working on issues regarding the conservation, research and restoration of the environment, formerly named the World Wildlife Fund, which remains its official name in Canada and the United States. It is the world's largest independent conservation organisation with over 5 million supporters worldwide, working in more than 90 countries, supporting around 1300 conservation and environmental projects around the world. It is a charity, with approximately 60 per cent of its funding coming from voluntary donations by private individuals. 45 per cent of the fund's income comes from the Netherlands, the United Kingdom and the United States.

- Wildlife conservation society
- Audubon society
- Traffic (conservation programme)
- Safari club international.

Bibliography

Botanical Survey of India. 1983. *Flora and Vegetation of India — An Outline*. Botanical Survey of India, Howrah. p. 24.

Classification of Organisms Wikipedia Kingdom (Biology).

Encyclopedia of World Geography by Peter Haggett.

Fungi of India 1989-2001, by Jamaluddin, M.G. Goswami and B.M. Ojha, Scientific Publishers, 2004, vii, 326 p, ISBN: 8172333544.

Threatened Birds of Asia, Accessed October 2006.

Tritsch, M.E. 2001. *Wildlife of India* Harper Collins, London. p. 192. ISBN 0-00-711062-6

Valmik Thapar, *Land of the Tiger: A Natural History of the Indian Subcontinent*, 1997.

Vivck Menon (2003). *A Field Guide to Indian Mammals*. Dorling Kindersley, Delhi. ISBN 0143029983.

Index

A

Amazon rainforest animals, 31, 32
Amazon basin, 62
Amazon pink river dolphin, 33
Amazon rain forest, 61
Amazon River, 62
Amazonian manatee, 33
Amphibians, 29
Anaconda, 34
Animal life in boreal forest, 35-42
- climate, 35-36
- indicator animal species
- main carnivores, 37-42
- plant species found, 36

Animals in rainforests biome, 26-34
- animals in rainforests, 28-29
- leafcutter ants, 30-31
- stick insects, 32
- strata of rainforest, 27-28
- tropical rainforest, 29
  - animal adaptations, 30
  - animals, 29-30

Animals in rainforests, 43-53
- amphibians, 44
- antbear, 47
- birds, 44
- black tree kangaroo, 48
- boas, 52
- common tree shrew, 49
- gorillas, 44, 46
- insects, 35
- jaguar, 51
- lesser Malay chevrotain, 47
- lizards, 44
- Malayan tapir, 51
- monkeys, 44
- ocelot, 47
- okapi, 48
- orang utan, 49
- other creatures, 44-46
- pangolin, 50
- pythons, 52
- reptiles, 44
- rhinoceros, 50
- siamang gibbon, 47
- slender loris, 51
- snakes, 52
- venomous species, 53

Animals living in forest habitat, 9-17

B

Biodiversity, 1, 54-80
- bioprospecting, 73-74
- driving forces of destruction, 64

fuel wood, 65
grazing land, 67
indigenous people, 75-80
leading the threat, 69-71
logging for tropical hardwoods, 64
paper industry, 65-66
rainforest pharmacy, 71-72
secrets of rainforests, 74
subsistence farming, 68
Birches, 42
Birds, 28, 29
Black caiman, 34

C

Capybara, 33

D

Dendrolagus ursinus, 48

E

Electric eel, 33
Elk, 38
Endangered animals, 111-139
African wild asses, 118-119
bald eafle, 126
beginning of life, 135
bespectacled bear, 134-135
bird of paradise, 124
black-footed ferret, 117
blue whale, 114-115
California condor, 127
gazelles, 120
giant anteater, 134
golden lion tamarin, 115
greater horseshoe bat, 111
ibexes, 130
Japanese ibis, 126
koalas, 131
Komodo dragon, 115, 122-123
leatherback turtles, 124
leopards, 119-120
lion-tailed macaque, 113
loggerhead turtle, 112
mandarin duck, 113
mountain gorilla, 114
musk oxen, 130
northern bald ibis, 112
numbat, 115
peregrine falcons, 129
Polar bears, 128-129
quetzal, 133
saving endangered animals, 138-139
scarlet macaw, 132
seladang, 123
soberian tiger, 111
spectacled bear, 116
Sumatran tiger, 121
takahe, 131
tapris, 123
white rhinoceros, 118
white tailed eagle, 112
Epiphytes, 2

F

Felis pardalis, 47
Forest ecosystem, 7-8

G

Gant sequoia, 37
Giant anteater, 32
Giant river otter, 32

Global warming, 102, 106
effects, 24
Golden lion tamarin, 32
Green algae, 31

H

Herbivores, 38
Hylobates syndactylus, 47

I

Illegal wildlife trade, 109
Importance of forests, 81-85
conserve soil, 83
keep environment pleasant, 82-83
main source of oxygen, 83
provide multiple benefits, 81-82
supply food, 84-85
Importance of rainforests, 59-61
Inorganic materials, 1
Insects, 28, 29
International Whaling Commission, 109
Introduction, 1-8

J

Jaguar, 34

K

L

Large cats, 45
Lecucaena leucocephala, 20
Logging, 40
Loss of forests, 100-110
cause of deforestation, 102
consequences of deforestation, 101
global warming, 102, 106
habitat loss, 107
motives of deforestation, 102
policies needed to halt deforestation, 104-105
Lycaon pictus, 19

M

Macaw, 33
Mammals, 28, 29

O

Okapia johnstoni, 48
Owl, 41

P

Piranha, 33
Poison arrow frog, 34
Pongo pygmaeus, 49
Porcupine, 40

R

Rainforest action, 58-59
Red deer, 38
Relationship between the people and forests, 86-93
Reptiles, 28, 29

S

Salvia, leucophylla, 20
Scarring and loss of diversity, 63
Sloth, 32
Snowshoe hare, 38
Species distribution, 18-25
abiotic and biotic factors, 22-23
clumped distribution, 18-20
grids projects, 23
random distribution, 21
regular or uniform distribution, 20

species distribution model, 21-22

Spider monkey, 32

T

Tragus javanicus, 47

Tupaia glis, 49

Types of forests, 3

boreal (taiga) forest, 6

temperate coniferous forest, 5-6

temperate deciduous forest, 4-5

tropical rainforest, 3-4

W

Wealth of rainforests, 57-58

Wildlife conservation, 140-148

Wildlife of India, 94-99

Z

Zaire, 114

Zosiac moth, 29